20th CENTURY
TIME
CAPSULE

This edition produced for
The Book People Ltd
Wood Avenue,
Haydock,
St Helens WA11 9UL

Produced by
Miles Kelly Publishing Ltd
Bardfield Centre, Great Bardfield, Essex, CM7 4SL

2 4 6 8 10 9 7 5 3 1

Project Manager: Kate Miles
Art Director: Clare Sleven
Designers: Angela Ashton, Geoff Sida
Assistants: Janice Bracken, Lesley Cartlidge, Ian Paulyn
Reprographics: DPI Colour Ltd

ISBN 1 85613 504 7

Printed in Singapore

20th CENTURY TIME CAPSULE

Philip Steele

TED SMART

Contents

INTRODUCTION

messages to the future

A GLIMPSE OF THE PAST

On 4 November 1922, an archaeologist called Howard Carter made a fantastic discovery in Egypt. It was the tomb of a young pharaoh, called Tutankhamun, who had come to the throne in about 1347BC. The tomb was packed with gold, as well as many everyday objects, such as chairs, beds, games, weapons, jewellery and clothes. It was a time capsule, which told later generations how people lived in ancient Egypt. Today, people sometimes mark a special date by making their own time capsule. They hope that in the future someone will find it and so learn about our own world. How could we best commemorate the last 100 years? This book gives you some suggestions...

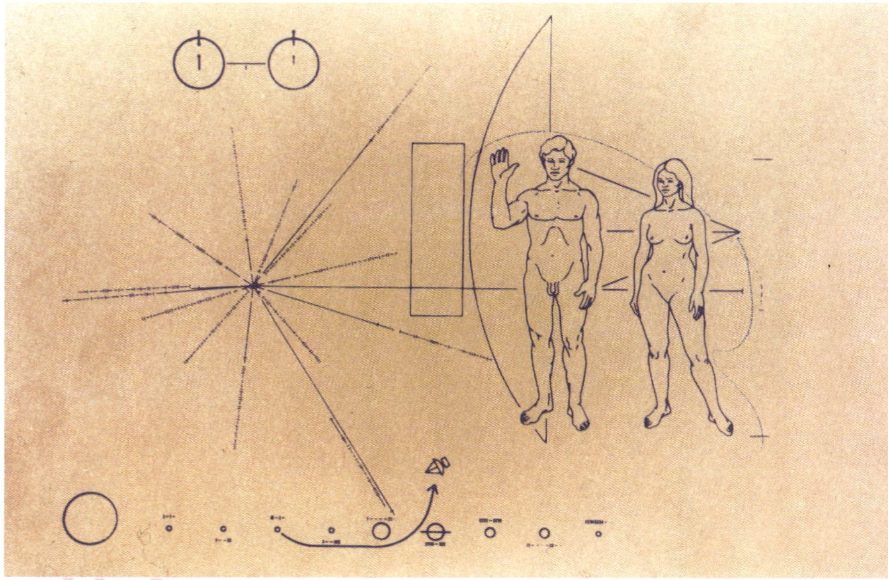

IS ANYBODY THERE?
This plaque was a kind of time capsule for outer space. It was put on the Pioneer space probes in the 1970s, to tell any intelligent life forms in outer space about human life and where to find it.

how to make your own time capsule

THE SECRET TUBE

A length of piping makes an ideal underground hiding place. Drainpipes and guttering are mostly made of light plastic, which is unlikely to remain waterproof when buried and may crack easily. You will need something rather more sturdy for your time capsule. Your local plumber's or Do-It-Yourself store should stock lengths of drainage pipe. These land or soil pipes will survive well underground and can be easily sealed. To do this you will need to buy two stop ends or access plugs – one for each end of the pipe. Place your items in the tube, stop off the ends and bury it in your chosen position.

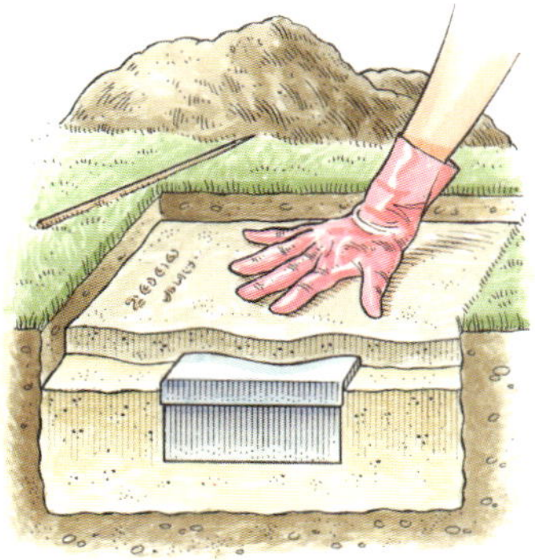

BURIED TREASURE

Pirates were said to bury their treasure in sea chests, but few of these seem to have survived. This storage method should be safer. First of all, find a biscuit tin. Then, dig a hole in the soil, allowing plenty of clearance for your tin on all sides. Mix up a cement, including a waterproofing agent. Fill the hole and then press the biscuit tin into the cement, making sure that it does not rise too high up the sides. Fill the box with your treasures and then put on the lid. Cover it with cement. While the cement is still wet, make hand prints (wearing rubber gloves!) and mark in the date with a pointed stick.

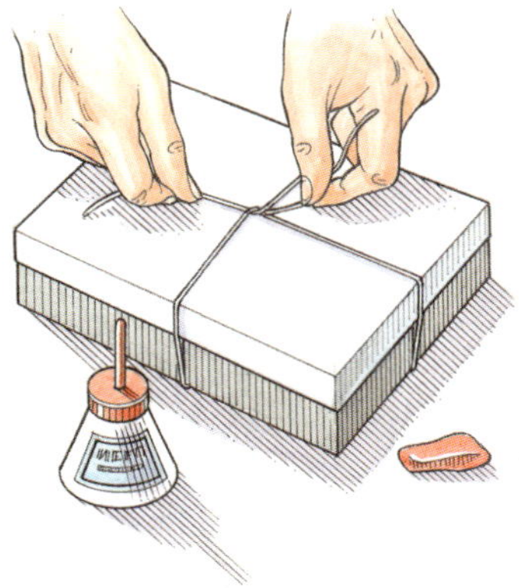

STRING AND SEALING WAX

You can probably think of many other items that would make excellent time capsules. An old vacuum flask would do very nicely. If you want to make your time capsule look attractive, you could use a strong wooden box. Seal the lid with PVA glue and then knot the outside with string or coloured cord. A few blobs of scarlet sealing wax would certainly intrigue whoever found it. You could press your initials in the wax before it dried. Of course, wood rots in damp places, but you could easily hide this time capsule in an attic or underneath floorboards.

ALL BRICKED UP

A small, flat tin would be ideal for placing inside a wall. Fill it with mementoes and close the lid firmly. Seal it with insulation tape. Many houses have cavity walls – two walls with a gap down the middle. That's a good place for your time capsule. We don't recommend knocking down your house! However if building repairs are being carried out, or an extension is being built, you may be able to brick up the tin. It could be hundreds of years before the wall is knocked down again and your tin is discovered. In the meantime, your time capsule could have become a valuable piece of history.

FAMILY

Imagine Christmas, 1900. A family gathers around the piano in the drawing room. Father stands by the fire, while mother sits at his side. Aunt plays the piano while uncle sings a sentimental song. Grandfather snoozes in an armchair. Five or six children and their cousins play outside, building a snowman. Over the century, scenes like this would change greatly, especially in North America or Europe. By the 1990s the typical family would be likely to have only two children. Relatives would be less likely to live in the same neighbourhood. The grandfather might be in an old people's home. And the Christmas entertainment? A compact disc player and computer games for the children.

THE FAMILY ALBUM
Cheap cameras made everyone a recorder of their own life and times. Keep some family photos for your time caspule.

CHANGING FAMILIES

During the late twentieth century, families became more fragmented, with divorce rates rising in the 1980s. More families were now being raised by a single parent.

WARTIME WEDDINGS

In the 1900s, weddings were very formal and marriages were expected to last. However courtship and family life were soon to be disrupted by two terrible wars. The First World War (1914-18) destroyed a generation of young men around the world. The Second World War (1939–45) uprooted families and left many homeless.

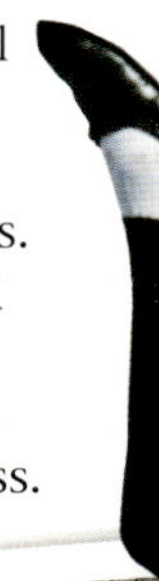

WATCH WITH MOTHER
The whole family gathers around one of the new television sets in the 1950s.

TIMELINE

1900

1906 Holiday camps for families

1907 Mother's Day

1910

1910 Father's Day

1912 Call for equality in divorce laws (UK)

1913 500,000 children ill or underfed in UK

1920

1920 Women vote in US federal elections

1920 World population 1,862 million

1923 A loaf of bread costs 200 billion Marks (Germany)

1930

1930 World population 2,070 million

1936 Marriage Bill (UK)

1939 Children evacuated from cities in case of war (UK)

1939 Citizens' Advice Bureau

1940

1940 World population 2,295 million

1940 Rationing, (UK)

1945 Family Allowance, (UK)

FAMILIES FROM AROUND THE WORLD

Family life has always varied greatly from one part of the world to another. In Saudi Arabia it is traditional for one man to have several wives, while in parts of the Himalayas one woman may have several husbands. In Borneo, dozens of families may live in the same 'longhouse'. Although birth rates have dropped in the west, they have risen in poorer countries. The world population rose from 1,633 million in 1900 to 5,926 million in 1998.

A CROWDED WORLD
The world's population is expected to double between 2000 and 2050.

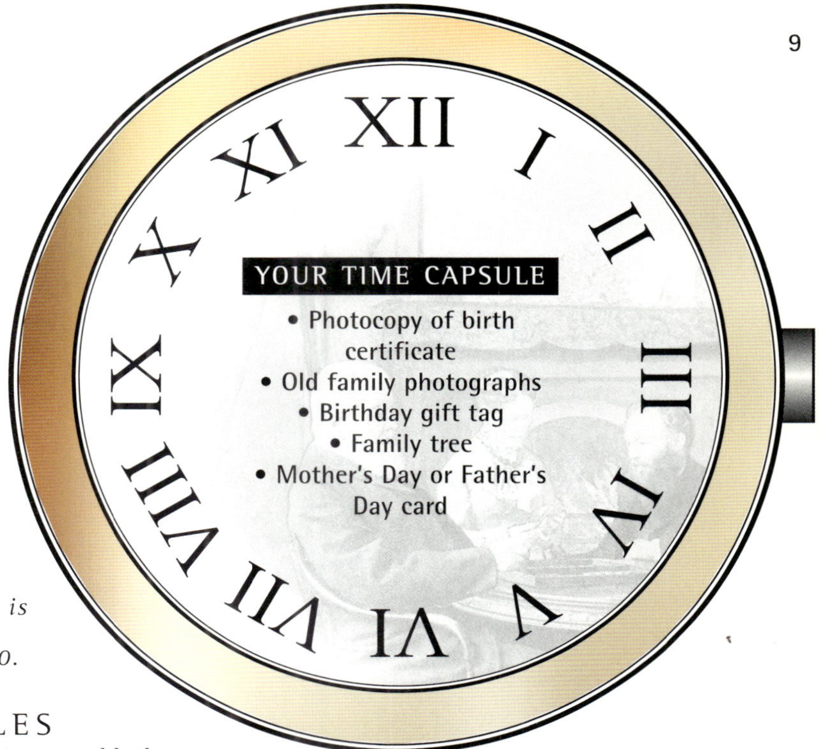

YOUR TIME CAPSULE

- Photocopy of birth certificate
- Old family photographs
- Birthday gift tag
- Family tree
- Mother's Day or Father's Day card

CHANGING ROLES

In many parts of the western world, the end of the twentieth century saw great changes in the parts played by men and women within the family. As more women went out to work, some men began to play a more active role in family life, looking after children, cooking and cleaning.

THE SKY'S THE LIMIT
A skydiving couple get married as they hurtle towards the ground. Wedding ceremonies have become less traditional as the century has progressed.

TIME FOR PLAY
From the 1960s, children were raised more informally than before.

950

950 World population ,515 million

951 Average UK housewife vorks 15-hour day

1960

1960 World population 3,019 million

1969 Peace and Music festival at Woodstock, USA

1970

1970 World population 3,698 million

1978 Test-tube baby (UK)

1980

1980 World population 4,450 million

1984 Frozen embryos (Australia)

1988 6,516 'Moonie' couples married in single ceremony (Korea)

1990

1990 World population 5,292 million

1998 Women worldwide can expect to live to 68, men to 64.

2000

HEALTH

In the 1900s, diseases such as tuberculosis and cholera claimed thousands of lives. Women and babies often died during childbirth. However by 1943 a new wonder drug called penicillin was being mass-produced. A World Health Organisation was set up in 1946. There were mass vaccinations. Housing and clean water supplies improved. More people could rely on free healthcare. Even so, many people around the world remained hungry and sick. Many were at risk from a new disease called AIDS which spread rapidly in the 1980s.

HOSPITAL HYGIENE
Hospitals were now kept clean and germ-free, even if they weren't always very comfortable.

ON CALL
A helicopter can often reach the scene of an accident within minutes.

EMERGENCY!

The first motor ambulance came into regular service in France, in 1900, replacing slow, uncomfortable horse-drawn carriages. By 1917, the first air ambulances were being used. Modern teams of paramedics, using high-speed motor ambulances or helicopters, are equipped to save lives on the spot.

KEEP FIT
Exercises first became popular in the 1930s. Today, many people work out at gyms or aerobic classes.

GOING INTO HOSPITAL

In the early 1900s, most hospitals were small and just served the local community. From the 1970s onwards, more very large hospitals were built, taking patients from a wider area. These hospitals needed to be fitted with expensive new equipment, such as brain scanners. As healthcare and medication improved, more and more people survived into old age and so wards became more crowded.

MIRACLE CURES
Pills and potions of the early 1900s were often ineffective. Later research did bring about genuine wonder drugs.

TIMELINE

1900

1901 Blood groups discovered (Austria)

1910

1914 Blood storage method

1918 Modern brain surgery (USA)

1920

1921 Insulin for diabetics (Canada)

1927 Iron lung (USA)

1928 Penicillium mould discovered (UK)

1930

1932 Anti scarlet fever drug (Germany)

1934 Radiotherapy (France)

1940

1940 Penicillin produced

1943 Kidney machine (Netherlands)

1943 Immune system discovered (UK)

1948 National Health Service

YOUR TIME CAPSULE

- Old prescription form
- Discarded medicine label only
- New sticking plaster
- Dental appointment card
- Gym membership card

HEALTHY LIFESTYLES

In 1910 a Polish chemist called Casimir Funk first used the word 'vitamins' to describe the chemicals which were found to occur naturally in healthy foods. By the 1970s we were being told that a varied diet and regular exercise were better for us than greasy hamburgers and sugary drinks in front of the television!

A MEDICAL REVOLUTION

The last 100 years have seen the greatest advances in medicine and surgery ever made. By 1967, even the human heart could be transplanted. Amazing new drugs and treatments are being invented all the time. However many doctors now believe that we use too many drugs such as antibiotics.

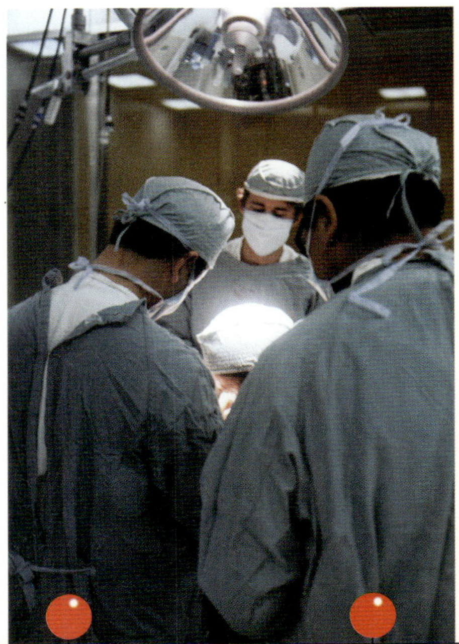

SURGICAL SKILLS

Surgeons can now see inside the human body with microscopic cameras and operate using laser beams. It is a far cry from the 1900s.

950 | 1960 | 1970 | 1980 | 1990 | 2000

950 Kidney transplant JSA)

954 Polio vaccine (USA)

958 Pacemaker for heart Sweden)

1960 Measles vaccine

1967 Heart transplant (S Africa)

1967 Start of worldwide anti-smallpox campaign

1971 CAT (brain) scanner (UK)

1973 Body scanner (UK)

1976 Eye operations with ultrasound (USA)

1982 Artificial heart (USA)

1983 Discovery of AIDS viruses

1990 Surgery on foetus (USA)

1990 Gene therapy (USA)

1995 AIDS cases exceed 1 million

FASHION

The last 100 years has seen a fashion revolution. You can no longer judge people's social class just from the clothes they wear. Today, even a princess can wear jeans and a T-shirt. In the 1900s, women wore long dresses, over uncomfortable corsets. The 1920s were more relaxed – and hemlines rose. By the 1960s the tiny miniskirt was in fashion and many women were finding trousers more practical. Men's clothes too became less formal and much more comfortable. Artificial fibres changed the way many clothes were made. For example nylon, patented in the USA in 1938, soon replaced cotton and silk for women's stockings. And the world centre of fashion design? In 1900, definitely Paris. In 1999? Paris still, but with the cities of London, Milan and New York as keen rivals.

STEPPING OUT
This is the 1900s style – top hats and frock coats.

IN THE PINK

Since the mid-1800s, men had tended to wear black for business. Their only really colourful clothes had been waistcoats, hunting jackets or army uniforms. In the 1920s, men began to wear more greys, browns, blue and checks. It was not until the 1960s that men started to dress like peacocks once again. Women had always worn colourful fashions. By the 1950s synthetic dyes were producing garish new colours. A young rock'n'roll fan might wear a full skirt of 'shocking' pink over her layers of starched petticoats.

AN ELEGANT AGE

During the 1900s, the upper and middle classes could afford to look respectable and affluent. Both men and women always left the house wearing hats and gloves. A fashionable lady might change her outfit several times during the day. Formal evening dress was always worn for dinner. This was still true in the 1930s, although by then daytime wear had been influenced by sporting clothes, such as tweed jackets and blazers.

READY FOR THE BALL
Permanent waves ('perms'), lipstick and face powder were all the rage from the 1920s into the 1950s.

FANCY THREADS
Knitting and sewing were useful hobbies which had become less popular by the 1980s.

TIMELINE

1900

1905 Zips manufactured (USA)

1909 Modern hair dyes

1910

1913 Modern brassière (France)

1919 Shorter hemlines (France)

1920

1920s The "Jazz Age" is time of the flapper – strapped, shoes, silk stockings, bobbed hair and short skirts.

1920 Hair drier (USA)

1930

1931 Longer skirts back in fashion

1933 Slacks popular for women

1938 Nylon stockings (USA)

1940

1942 Wartime 'utility' fashions

1946 Bikini (France)

1947 Dior's 'New Look' (France)

THE SIXTIES

The 1960s formed a turning point in the history of fashion. Girls no longer wanted to look elegant or dress in good taste. They wanted to look outrageous and modern. They wanted to be noticed. By 1965, miniskirts were being worn 15 centimetres above the knee.

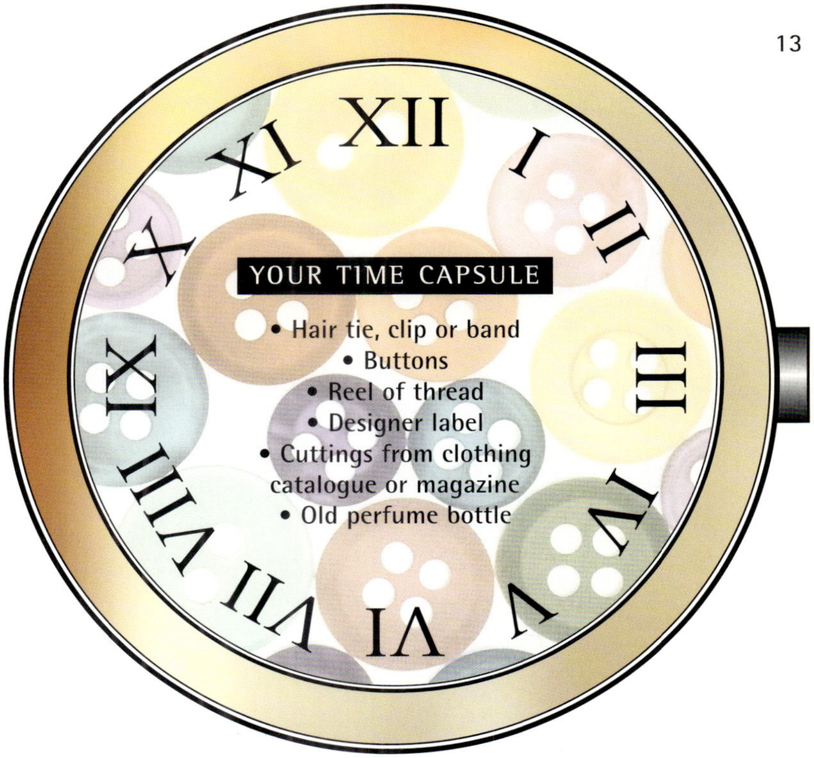

SHOCK VALUE

In the early 1970s, fashions for men and women became romantic, using fabrics such as velvet and cotton. The reaction came later in the 70's. 'Punks' wore torn clothes, leather, chains and studs. Their bodies were pierced and their hair might be pink or green.

NAMED BRANDS

In the 1980s and 90s the designer label became all-important. School children just had to have the right brand name on their expensive trainers. T-shirts, popular since the 1960s, became advertising billboards. Trainers and T-shirts became the height of fashion.

LET'S DANCE!
The 1960s look made use of fabrics such as shiny plastics, metal and leather. Clothing and jewellery were based on simple, geometric designs. Women wore leather boots, often to the knee.

PUNK AND FASHION
At first, punk fashions caused shock or laughter. But soon all sorts of people were piercing ears and noses.

THE TRAINER
A sports shoe or a fashion item? It no longer mattered.

950

953 'Stiletto' high heels

955 Blue jeans for vomen

955 Boned bathing ostumes for women.

1960

1962 Yves St Laurent couture

1965 Miniskirt (UK/France)

1966 Hippie fashion

1969 Maxi skirt

1970

1971 Hot pants

1974 Menswear by Georgio Armani

1976 Punk fashion

1980

1980 New Romantic look

1984 Karl Lagerfield collection

1989 Eco-friendly fashion

1990

1992 'Grunge' look

1997 Death of Gianni Versace

2000

HOBBIES

Leisure was king in the twentieth century. Although there were some periods of hardship, more workers now enjoyed paid holidays. Saturday often became a free day in addition to Sunday, creating the 'weekend'. By the 1950s, even teenagers had enough money in their pockets to buy records or go dancing. Younger children enjoyed crazes for particular toys. The yo-yo, a spinning disc which was already popular in ancient Greece, became the fad of the 1930s – and the 1950s and the 1990s!

Long winter evenings might be spent model-making on the kitchen table, or sticking collections of stamps into albums. People collected all sorts of things, from matchboxes to cigarette cards featuring pictures of their sporting heroes.

DIG THAT JIVE!
Out of the jitterbugging '40s came the jiving 50s and the golden age of rock'n'roll.

DANCE CRAZY

If you danced the waltz in the 1900s, you were in for a rude awakening in the years that followed. Wild jazz music was first created by African American bands in the city of New Orleans at the start of the century. It caught on around the world and was followed by all kinds of variants and dance crazes, from the 'Roaring 20s' onwards. Swing and jitterbug dancing kept up spirits during the Second World War (1939-45).

Latin dances such as the tango, rumba and samba also remained firm favourites. The craze of the 1950s was rock'n'roll, which went on to take the world by storm. The popular music scene reached the height of its energy in the 1960s, with new inspiration coming from Britain and the Caribbean. Punk, disco, techno... the world kept dancing.

ANYONE FOR BRIDGE?
Card games were always popular, as well as boardgames such as Monopoly (1933) and Scrabble (1948)

TIMELINE

1900

1900 Meccano (UK)

1901 Kodak cameras (USA)

1910

1910 Girl Guides founded (UK)

1913 Newspaper crosswords (UK)

1913 Chelsea Flower Show

1917 Electric hand drill (DIY)

1920

1921 First radio sports commentary

1924 Crossword puzzle mania hits USA.

1925 35-mm Leica camera

1930

1930 Pinball machine (USA)

1933 Monopoly (USA)

1940

1943 Adventure playground (Denmark)

1948 Frisbee flying disc (USA)

1948 Scrabble (USA)

ACOUSTIC GUITAR
Folksinger's favourite.

NEVER A DULL MOMENT

In the 1950s, the guitar began to replace the piano as the most popular musical instrument to be played in the home. By the 1960s, the electric guitar, loud and shiny, was every teenager's dream of the perfect birthday present. Table tennis bats and tables were to be found in many a garage. Weekend trips to the swimming pool kept many families fit. By the 1980s, gardening and Do-it-Yourself had become hugely popular weekend activities for the adults in the family.

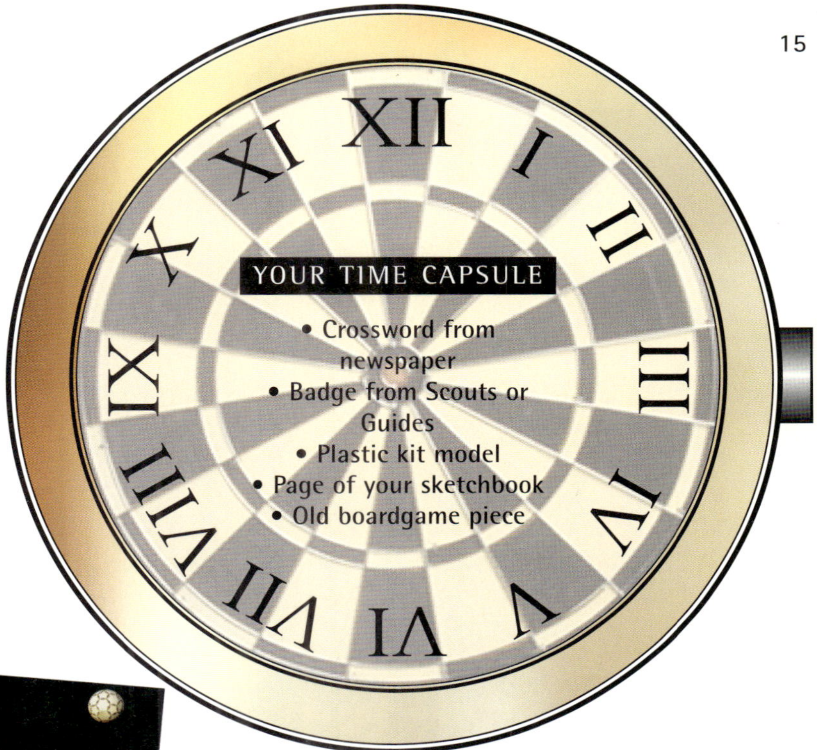

YOUR TIME CAPSULE

- Crossword from newspaper
- Badge from Scouts or Guides
- Plastic kit model
- Page of your sketchbook
- Old boardgame piece

OVER HERE!
By the 1990s, girls were forming their own football teams, just as boys had done for years.

CYBER GAMES

The first ever video game was invented in the United States in 1972. During the 1980s, computer games became more realistic. In the 1990s, the Internet, a worldwide computer communications network, provided new opportunities for games in 'cyberspace'.

TOYS OF OUR TIME
What would these models tell people in the future? That we were excited by the idea of space travel, but still loved heroic and romantic story lines.

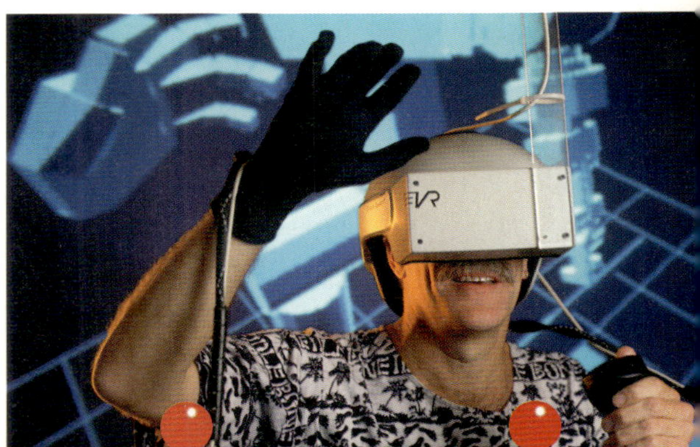

VIRTUAL REALITY
No joystick, no key-boards – you are in the game.

950

55 Lego plastic toy
lding (Denmark)

58 Hula hoop craze (USA)

1960

1960 Chubby Checker's hit *Let's Twist Again*, starts dance craze

1963 Polaroid camera

1970

1972 Video game (USA)

1979 Rubik's Cube puzzle (Hungary)

1980

1981 Trivial Pursuit boardgame (Canada)

1983 Compact Disc players (CDs) on sale

1990

1996 Collecting madness – one postage stamp sold for £1,420,000

2000

SPORT

In 1996, no less than *138.5 million* fans of American football turned on their televisions to watch one event – the Super Bowl! This was the century of sport, from athletics to tennis, from soccer to baseball. During the early 1900s, many sports set up new leagues and international contests. Spectators flocked to see ball games, or watch new fangled racing cars speed around dirt tracks. By the 1920s, people were following their favourite sports on radio and, by the 1950s, on television. Sporting records fell again and again, as athletes pushed themselves to new limits. Sport was supreme. But by the 1960s it had become big business – and, said the old-timers, less fun. Even so, more people than ever were now taking part in sports themselves.

YELLING FOR THE TEAM
American football started off as a college game in the United States in the 1870s. Its origins lay in the British games of rugby and soccer.

AN EYE ON THE BALL

American football first became established as a 'pro' game in the 1920s, with the founding of the National Football League (NFL). The colourful history of the NFL has been sprinkled with great stars like Ernie Nevers, who in 1927 scored 40 points in a single game. Then there was George Blanda, who notched up 340 games in 26 seasons (1949-75). Now the game has an international following and the hugely popular Superbowl league games are watched on television by many millions of viewers worldwide.

WORLD'S FAVOURITE GAME
Soccer 1910 style. English team Blackburn Rovers takes on Aston Villa.

ROLLING ALONG
Roller-skating was a craze at the start of the century. Four-wheel metal skates (below) were strapped on to the shoe.

TIMELINE

1900

1903 Tour de France cycle race

1906 French Grand Prix

1910

1910 Sand yachting (Belgium)

1911 Indianapolis 500 (motor racing)

1917 National Hockey League (Canada)

1920

1922 Water-skiing (USA)

1924 International Ski Federation

1922 1st World Professional Snooker Championship

1930

1930 Soccer World Cup held in Uruguay

1932 International Basketball Federation founded

1936 Jesse Owens (USA) wins 4 Olympic gold medals

1940

1940 Ice hockey on TV (USA

1942 French soccer player scores 16 goals in one match

1947 International Volleyball Association founded

A GO-ANYWHERE CYCLE

Mountain bikes first appeared in the USA in the 1970s. They were designed for toughness rather than speed, with a very robust frame. The large number of gears made it possible to tackle very steep slopes. The tyre treads were chunky, for gripping in wet or icy conditions. There was extra clearance between the wheels and the forks, to allow for thick mud. Even if you never went near a mountain, they were fun to ride!

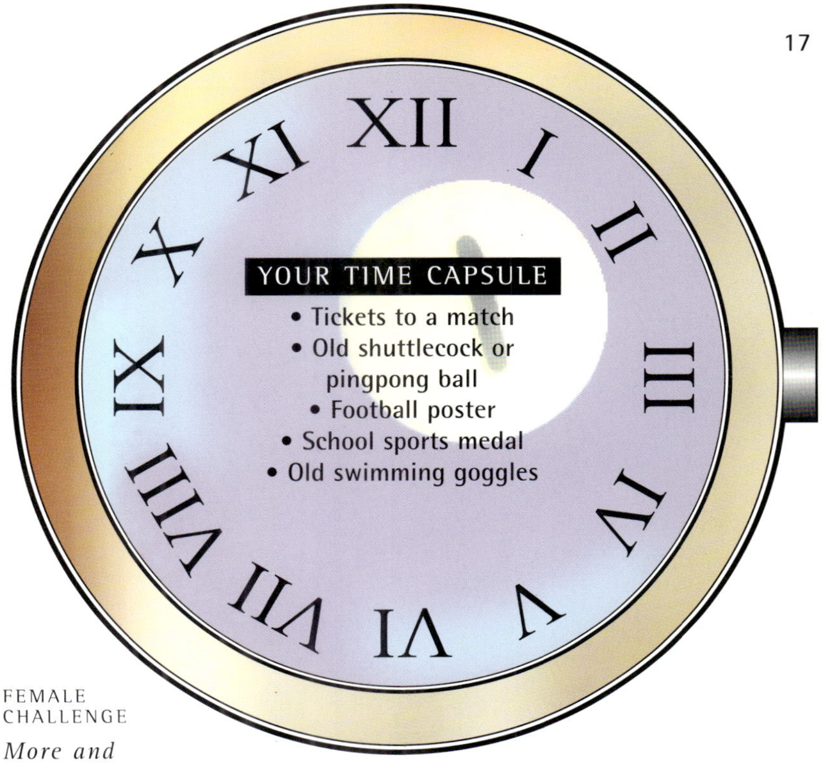

YOUR TIME CAPSULE

- Tickets to a match
- Old shuttlecock or pingpong ball
- Football poster
- School sports medal
- Old swimming goggles

HARD ROCK

Outdoor pursuits became very popular in the 1980s and 90s, and many people took up sports that provided a personal challenge such as rock climbing, canoeing or windsurfing, rather than team sports.

FEMALE CHALLENGE

More and more girls and women have taken up rock climbing in recent years. Many have excelled at this sport.

SPORTSWEAR

The modern hurdler wears tight-fitting shorts to reduce wind resistance and trainers for maximum grip with the track.

NEW SPORTS

First of all there were skateboards, which were a cross between a surfboard and roller skates. And then there were snowboards, a cross between skateboards and skis. They are shaped rather like a mini-surfboard, with bindings to secure the feet. Snowboarding soon became the sport for cool young people.

SNOWBOARD ANTICS

It's the 1990s, and extreme acrobatics are taking over.

950

50 Biggest soccer crowd 199,854 (Brazil)

51 International Judo deration founded

56 Plastic foam rfboards (USA)

1960

1960 Golfer Jack Nicklaus wins his 1st US Open

1963 Lacoste patent steel tennis racquet

1964 Tokyo Olympics

1970

1972 Swimmer Mark Spitz (USA) wins 7 medals in one Olympics

1973 Mountain bikes (USA)

1976 World hang-gliding championships

1980

1987 First Rugby World Cup

1988 Fastest men's marathon time – 2 hr 6mn 56 sec

1990

1990 Tennis star Martina Navratilova wins Wimbledon for record 9th time

1995 Highest cricket innings (Brian Lara, 501 not out)

2000

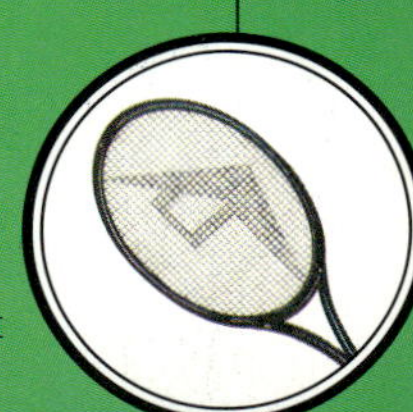

BUILDINGS

RED BRICK TERRACES

Terraced housing in Great Britain may have lacked privacy and space, but it did foster a sense of community. In the days before motor traffic became heavy, children could safely play in the streets.

THE SKYSCRAPER

In the late 1800s, European engineers had experimented with tall structures of iron and steel. But it was in Chicago and New York City that high-rise architecture really took off, in the early 1900s. New York's Singer Building of 1908 was 187 metres high, but by 1974 Chicago's Sears Tower broke the record at 443 metres. By 1996, the world's tallest office block was on the other side of the world, in Kuala Lumpur, Malaysia. The twin Petronas Towers soared to 452 metres.

In the 1800s, architects often looked back to the days of ancient Rome or the Middle Ages when they designed public buildings. After the 1900s many architects tried instead to build exciting new cities made of steel, glass and concrete. In American cities, buildings reached dizzying new heights. Stairs? No problem! From 1908 onwards electric lifts were designed which could do the serious climbing for you. Soon skyscrapers were appearing in cities around the world. They weren't always popular, however. They dwarfed beautiful old buildings in city centres and large areas of concrete sometimes looked the worse for wear after a few years. High-rise buildings were not much loved as homes, either. Tall blocks of flats were built all over the world in the 1960s, but they weren't really built on a human scale. The people who lived in them soon missed chatting to their neighbours over the garden wall.

TIMELINE

1900

1908 Singer Building, NYC 187 m

1910

1913 Woolworth Building, NYC 241m

1919 Bauhaus architecture (Germany)

1920

1926 Architect Antonio Gaudi (Spain) dies.

1928 de Stijl architecture (Netherlands)

1930

1930 Chrysler Building, NYC 319m

1931 Empire State Building, NYC 381m

1940

1943 Start of Guggenheim Museum, NYC

1945 Much of Europe lies bombed

FLOWER POWER
Psychedelic designs influenced homes and even cars in the 1960s (left).

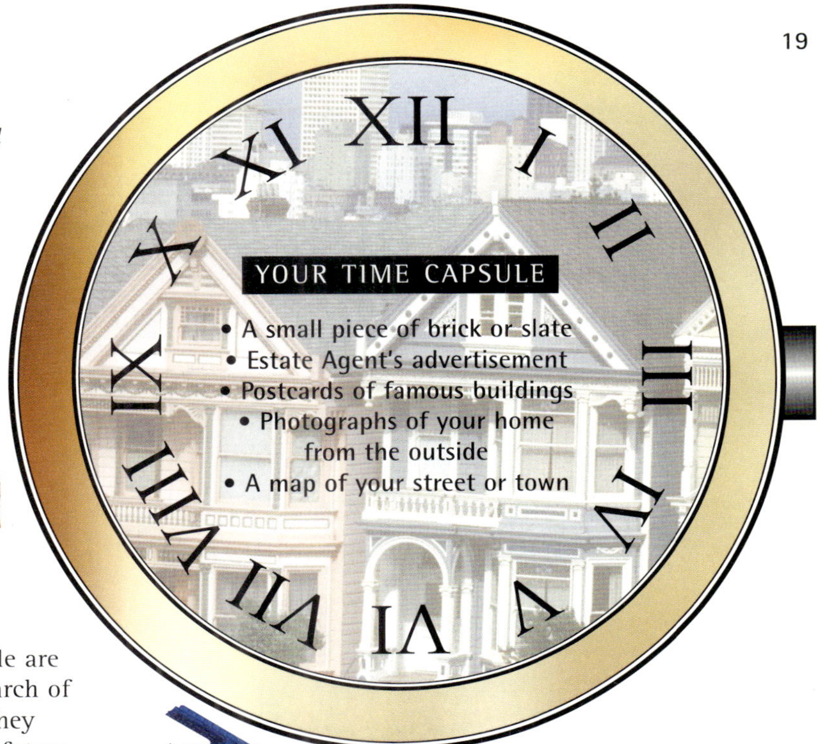

YOUR TIME CAPSULE

- A small piece of brick or slate
- Estate Agent's advertisement
- Postcards of famous buildings
- Photographs of your home from the outside
- A map of your street or town

HOMES OF THE WORLD

Before the 1900s, most buildings in the world were made of local materials, such as stone, clay, timber or turf. In the twentieth century, it became easier to transport building materials over longer distances, and so many cities around the world began to look much the same. In 1901 architects began to experiment with building methods, using prefabricated concrete sections, prepared in a factory and then assembled on site. However regional styles of architecture may still be seen in many parts of the world today, from thatched huts in Africa to the reed houses of Iraq's Marsh Arabs. Many of these are much better suited to the local climate and conditions than the 'modern' buildings which are replacing them.

CITIES OF THE FUTURE

All over the world, people are pouring into cities in search of work and a better life. They rarely find either. In the future, all cities must be carefully planned and built on a more human scale. Key problems to solve include pollution, public transport and services. In the 1970s many city centres became run down. These need to be brought back to life – cities are for living in as well as working.

SAILS IN STONE
Sydney Opera House, Australia, was opened in 1973.

CITYSCAPE
Lloyd's building in London's City district, symbol of a new era.

MILLENNIUM VISION
What kind of cities will we need in the next 1,000 years? Will we need cities at all?

950

950 United Nations
eadquarters, New York

952 Unité d'Habitation, Le
orbusier

1960

1960 New congress building, Brasilia

1965 Gateway to West arch, St Louis

1970

1973 World Trade Centre, NYC 415m

1974 Sears Tower Chicago 443m

1977 Pompidou Centre, Paris

1980

1980 Shenzhen, China, fastest growing city

1984 World's tallest mosque (Morocco)

1989 World's biggest church (Ivory Coast)

1990

1996 Petronas Towers, Malaysia (452m)

1997 Massive rebuilding programme, Berlin

2000

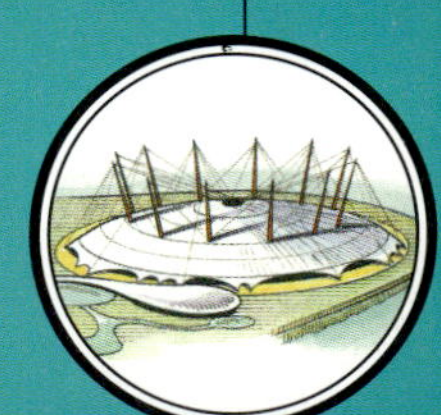

INTERIORS

Many people who lived through the twentieth century would say that their lives were changed more by the arrival of water mains and electricity than by any other event. At the start of the century, a large number of people in the western world still lived in appalling city slums or primitive country cottages, lit by oil or gas lamps and with water coming from a pump in the yard. Today housing and services have improved hugely, although they remain desperate in many of the world's poorer countries. In the 1900s, many houses were still dark and cluttered, with heavy curtains, blinds and screens to keep out the draughts. In the 1920s and 30s, houses became lighter. Kitchens became more streamlined, with hygienic work surfaces and built in cupboards. In the 1900s, coal fires were normal, with central heating only in grand houses. It did not become widespread until the 1950s.

COOL IT!
Refrigerators were invented in 1913 and became popular between the 1930s and 50s.

FURNITURE CHANGES STYLE

The Victorians liked heavy ornate furniture, made of polished hardwoods. Their wardrobes, chests of drawers and overstuffed armchairs remained widely used during the first half of the century. However in the 1920s, German and Dutch designers brought in a new look. Styles became simpler and more practical, more modern. By the 1950s the influence of new technologies was to be seen in the home, with fitted carpets made of synthetic fibres, plastic lampshades, and the new television set taking pride of place in the sitting room.

BATHTIME
It was only during this century that proper bathrooms and indoor toilets were fitted in most homes.

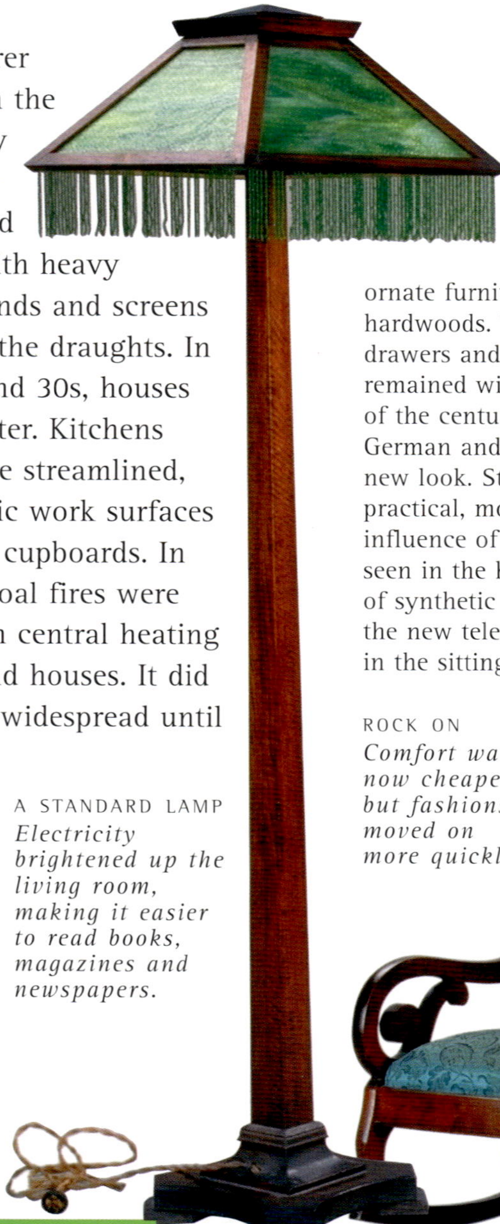

A STANDARD LAMP
Electricity brightened up the living room, making it easier to read books, magazines and newspapers.

ROCK ON
Comfort was now cheaper, but fashions moved on more quickly.

TIMELINE

1900

1901 Electric vacuum cleaner

1902 Automatic tea maker (UK)

1910

1910 Bathroom scales

1911 Air conditioning (USA)

1919 Bauhaus school of design (Germany)

1920

1923 Electric kettle (UK)

1923 Electric refrigerators

1927 Electric blanket (UK)

1930

1935 Fluorescent lighting (USA)

1938 Invention of Teflon

1938 Nylon bristles for toothbrushes

1940

1940 Automatic swing doors

1943 Telephone answering machine

1947 First microwave ovens

THE HOUSEWIFE
In the 1950s, a woman's place was still in the kitchen – but for how much longer?

HOUSEWORK MADE EASY

In the 1900s, upper and middle class families had servants. They cooked the meals, washed the clothes, beat the carpets, scrubbed the steps and cleaned the silver. During the years that followed, more and more inventions made housework easier. The electrical vacuum cleaner was invented in 1901, the electric toaster in 1909 and the steam iron in 1938. Electric washing machines appeared in 1915 and were fully automated by 1939. It took many years for these appliances to catch on, The microwave oven was invented in 1945 but was not marketed until 1967 or widely used until the 1980s.

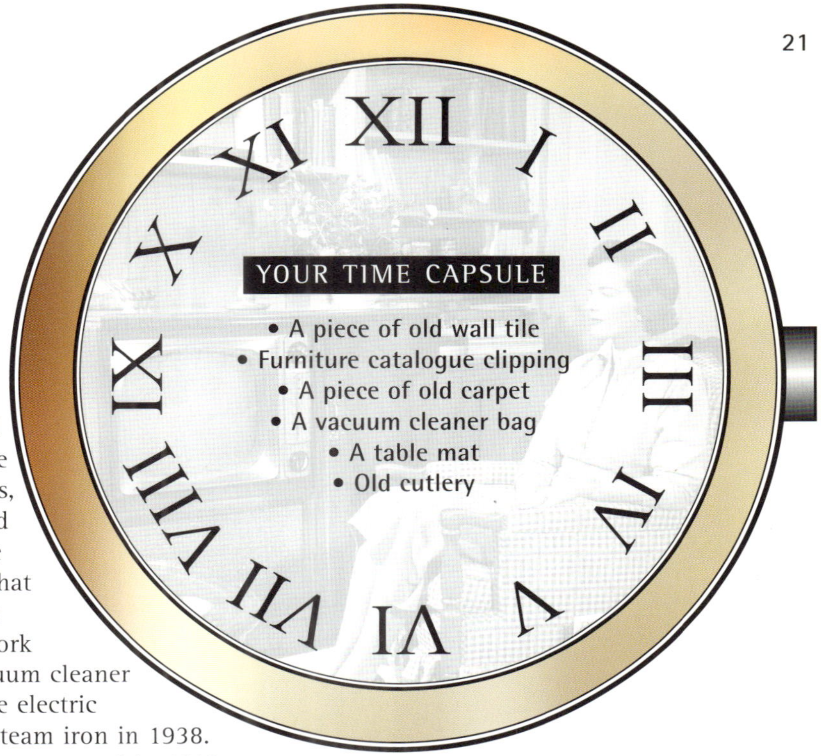

HI-TECH KITCHEN
The post-modern kitchen of the 1990s.

ROOM SET
In the 1970s clean lines and bright colours were used in decorating the home.

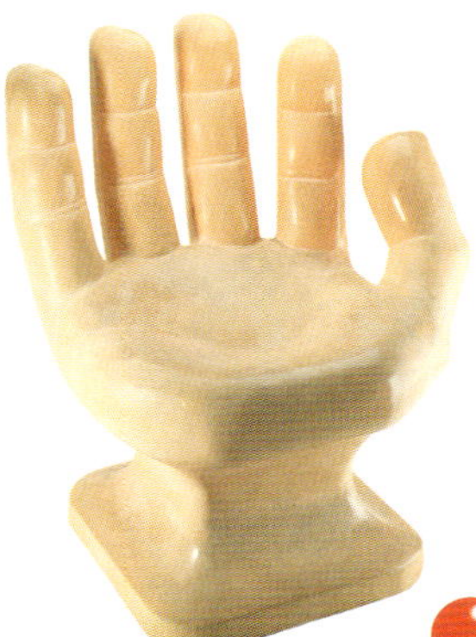

FUN DESIGN
Moulded plastics could be used for all sorts of fantastic and silly designs, like this 1970s chair.

950

58 Modern fan heater
rmany) Unité
Iabitation, Le Corbusier

1960

1965 Swiss architect Le Corbusier, dies

1968 Roy Jacuzzi markets whirlpool baths

1970

1972 First video cassette recorder

1972 *Pong*, first computer game, launched

1974 First personal computer (PC)

1980

1981 Memphis design group founded

1984 Lloyds building finished, London

1990

1993 Voice-operated TV remote control

2000

TRANSPORT

ACROSS THE SKY
Many aircraft of the 1900s were biplanes, having double wings.

HOLIDAY BOUND!
Steam trains in the 1950s fill with holiday passengers.

The first powered flight took place in the American state of North Carolina 1903, when the Wright brothers' Flyer I lurched over a distance of just 36 metres. By 1969 the first supersonic passenger aircraft, Concorde, could fly from Paris to New York in under 3.5 hours! This was the century in which our planet shrank. One new form of transport after another made it possible to travel around the world more rapidly. It was the age of airships, hovercraft, jets, high-speed trains, aerofoils. The ultimate dream came true in 1961, when a human being first left Earth to travel in space. However transport in this century was not just for the adventurous or rich. The first really popular family car was the Model T Ford. An incredible 18 million of these were produced from 1908 to 1927. Motoring brought personal freedom – but at what cost to the environment?

HAPPY MOTORING
The Ford Anglia was a cheap family car, popular in the UK in the 1960s.

SCOOTER POWER
The motor scooter became very popular in Italy in the 1950s. In the 1960s, it became the favourite of Britain's youth gangs, known as 'Mods'.

ON THE RAILWAYS

Steam power reached its peak in the 1930s, but by the 1950s steam locomotives were being replaced by diesel electrics. In the 1960s, new high-speed trains were developed in Japan and France

TIMELINE

1900

1900 Hydrofoil (Italy)

1908 Model T Ford (USA)

1910

1910 Seaplane (France)

1912 Diesel locomotive (Germany)

1914 Traffic lights (USA)

1920

1921 Motorway (Germany)

1923 Autogiro (early helicopter, Spain)

1927 Solo trans-Atlantic flight (USA-France)

1930

1930 Jet engine (UK)

1935 Parking meter (USA)

1936 Volkswagen 'beetle' (Germany)

1940

1941 Jeep (USA)

1947 Supersonic aircraft (USA)

1948 Citroën 2cv (France)

DOUBLE DECKERS

Double-decker buses were popular in British cities and were exported to British colonies such as Hong Kong (a part of China since 1997).

YOUR TIME CAPSULE

- Old bus pass
- Used airline or ferry ticket
- A train or bus timetable
- A model car
- A road map
- Old bicycle stickers

PUBLIC TRANSPORT

The transport revolution speeded up dramatically in the 1900s with the mass production of motor buses and the use of electricity to power underground trains and trams. More and more people lived in city suburbs and relied on public transport to get to work. By the 1970s, private car ownership was growing rapidly and better public transport seemed the only away to prevent bigger traffic jams.

NEW DESTINATIONS

Transport changes the way we live in all sorts of ways. The railways encouraged people to leave their homes for the first time, for day trips to the seaside. The motorcar made it as easy for people to tour the countryside as to stay in a hotel in a large resort. In the 1960s, cheap air flights allowed ordinary people to holiday abroad in sunny countries. By the 1990s tourists were even visiting Antarctica.

HOVERING

The hovercraft, which rides on a cushion of air, was invented in Britain in 1956.

TRAINS A GRANDE VITESSE

The French TGVs developed in the 1970s and 80s could top 380 km per hour.

SUN POWER

Is solar energy the fuel of the future? Solar-powered cars, boats and aircraft have been built since the 1980s.

950

955 Nuclear-powered ubmarine (USA)

959 Mini Minor (UK)

1960

1964 Bullet train (Japan)

1969 Concorde supersonic passenger jet (UK/France)

1969 Boeing 747 'Jumbo' Jet

1970

1970 Flight simulators for training pilots (USA)

1976 Air speed of almost 3,530kph (USA)

1980

1982 Railed rocket sled reaches 9,851kph (USA)

1985 First commercial UK/Australia flight for *Concorde*

1990

1990 Motorcycle exceeds 518kph (USA)

2000

EDUCATION

Before the 1900s, many poor children received little education. By the end of the century, there was free schooling for all and children from many different backgrounds could go on to college or university. It was a great advance. Teaching methods also changed. In the 1900s pupils often had to learn lists and poems and multiplication tables off by heart.

School rules were very strict and children were often punished. By the 1960s, the emphasis had changed. Pupils were now encouraged to find things out for themselves and to work in teams. Schools were more relaxed and informal. But was there still enough formal, old-fashioned education? And how should schools be funded? These questions were argued about over and over again in the 1990s.

PLEASE MISS!
The old-fashioned classroom – rows of desks face a blackboard.

WHAT DID YOU LEARN IN SCHOOL TODAY?

In the 1900s, elementary schools concentrated on reading, writing and arithmetic. Other schools taught Latin and Greek, one modern language, grammar, mathematics, history, and geography. All university students would be expected to have a good knowledge of Latin.

ALL ALIKE?
School uniforms were worn in many countries. A good idea?

HIGH SCHOOL BUS
US schoolgirls catch the bus, 1950 style. Education was now seen as a right for all.

TIMELINE

1900

1902 Council-run schools (UK)

1907 Montessori school (Italy)

1910

1912 IQ tests

1918 School leaving age raised to 14 (UK)

1920

1924 First BBC broadcast on radio (UK)

1930

1932 First educational television programme (USA)

1940

1945 Free education for all, school-leaving age raised to

1946 Outward bound school (UK)

1948 Comprehensive schools planned (UK)

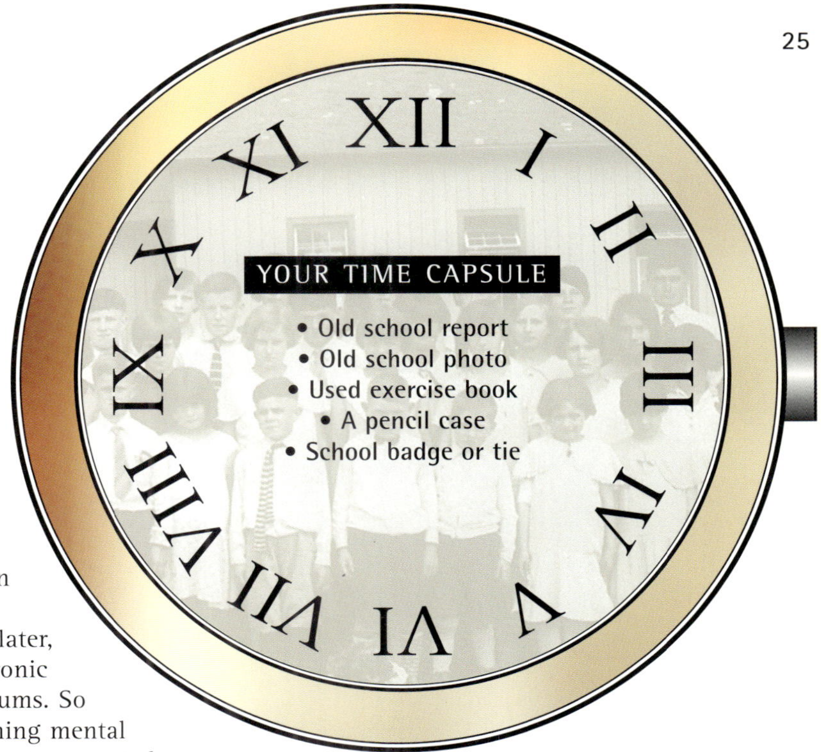

YOUR TIME CAPSULE

- Old school report
- Old school photo
- Used exercise book
- A pencil case
- School badge or tie

WHO GOES WHERE?

Churches ran many schools, with monks and nuns as teachers. In some countries, most children went to state-run schools. In others, private schools were favoured by the wealthy. In Britain, these were – rather confusingly – called 'public' schools. There were divisions within the state system, too, with the British 'grammar school', the German *Gymnasium* or the French *lycée* following a more academic timetable. Comprehensive education – one school for all – was introduced in many countries in the 1950s.

SCHOOLS FOR TOFFS?
Schoolboys from Eton, Britain's top 'public' school, formed a social elite – and still do today.

TEACH FOR TOMORROW?

In the 1950s, children practised solving sums in their heads – 'mental arithmetic'. Thirty years later, children could use electronic calculators to do these sums. So should they still be learning mental arithmetic? New technology presented schools with many such problems. By the 1990s, children clearly needed to learn computer skills. But just how effective were computers as teaching aids? They were no substitute for a good teacher!

A FAIRER SYSTEM?
Comprehensive education aimed to give all children an equal start in life.

ELECTRONIC EDUCATION
In the 1990s, there was a great drive to give schools access to more computers.

950

951 GCE exams

954 US Supreme Court
ules that segregation by
ce in public schools is
nconstitutional

1960

1963 Great increase in university education (UK)

1968 Student riots, Paris

1969 Open University (UK)

1970

1973 School leaving age raised to 16 (UK)

1976 All secondary schools comprehensive (UK)

1980

1987 GCSE exams (UK)

1988 National Curriculum (UK)

1990

1997 OFSTED inspections begin – primary and secondary schools (UK)

2000

FOOD

THE GROCER'S

New chain stores appeared on the high street in the 1900s. They still served each customer individually and delivered groceries to the home – by bicycle.

In the 1900s, family meals were held at regular times and were very formal. Much of the food was purchased from small, local suppliers. Most dishes were home-made. Rich people could afford cooks and hold dinner parties, but many poor people went hungry. As the years went by, people ate more and more processed foods. These were easy to prepare but were not always very healthy. Supermarkets appeared in the United States in the 1930s and spread to Europe in the 1950s. There were big changes in food production. There were new fertilisers, new strains of wheat, new pesticides and machines. Some new farming methods proved disastrous, but crop yields slowly increased. By the 1970s the world's fertile lands were producing too much food, while people living in the dry lands of Africa were starving.

CHOCOLATE TIME

The twentieth century had a sweet tooth. Put a chocolate wrapper in your time capsule.

PACKAGING AND ADVERTISING

Already at the start of the century, food manufacturers were realising the importance of brand names, packaging and catchy slogans. With the arrival of radio advertising (as early as 1922 in the United States) and commercial television (1941), the war of the food companies began in earnest. By the 1990s the big advertisers were supermarket chains, who were driving many smaller shops from the high street.

TABLE MANNERS

Sit up straight, don't talk with your mouth full, don't eat too quickly...

DRINK YOUR MILK

Homogenised milk had the cream mixed in. Pasteurised milk was heated to kill off germs.

TIMELINE

1900

1901 Instant coffee (Japan)

1907 Canned tuna fish

1910

1913 Coca-Cola bottle (USA)

1920

1921 Famine in Russia

1922 Tinned baby food (USA)

1922 Choc-ice (USA)

1923 A loaf of bread costs 200 billion Marks (Germany)

1930

1930's Soya as meat substitute

1933 Lyons Corner House (UK)

1935 d. Auguste Escoffier, great French chef

1940

1946 Freeze-dried food (USA

1946 Espresso coffee machin (Italy)

1947 Food processor (UK)

1948 Macdonald hamburgers (USA)

FRESH FROM THE LAND
The variety of food on the market increased greatly after the widespread shortages of the Second World War.

YOUR TIME CAPSULE

- Ingredients list from food packaging
- List of your favourite meals
- Washed milk or juice carton
- Menu from Take-away restaurant
- A recipe from a magazine
- An old egg-timer

BARBECUED!
Outdoor cooking was an institution in Australia and the USA.

PRESERVING FOOD

Frozen food first went on sale in the USA in 1930 and soon became popular. People were more suspicious in the 1990s when biologists changed the genes of tomatoes to give them a longer shelf life.

YOUR TABLE, MADAM
Eating out became a favourite way of celebrating or relaxing.

A WORLD OF TASTES

In the 1960s more and more people began to eat out at restaurants. The classic French restaurants remained popular, but soon westerners were experimenting with delicious tastes from all over the world – Italy, Spain, Eastern Europe, India, China and Southeast Asia. The chief American contribution was 'fast food' – rapidly prepared snacks. Most popular of all was the hamburger, which by the 1980s was being eaten all over the world.

COOKING FOR PLEASURE
By the 1990s cooking had become a popular hobby for both men and women. Television programmes inspired them to be adventurous. The supermarkets now stocked many foreign foods.

950

951 Milk carton (Sweden)

956 Clarence Birdseye, ıventor of process for deep-reezing food, dies

1960

1962 Beer cans with tabs introduced in USA

1964 Long-life milk

1970

1976 Phrase 'junk food' first used

1978 Magimix food processor introduced

1980

1982 Diet Coke launched in USA

1985 Launch of Live Aid to relieve starving in Ethiopia

1990

1996 Genetically modified soya beans

2000

WRK

A hundred years ago, many people still worked on the land. Soon, more and more farm work was being done by machines, so workers moved into factories in the big cities. Here too there were big changes. Production lines were making manufacture much faster and more efficient. At the same time old craft skills were being lost and work often became boring and repetitive. Trade unions faced a long struggle to improve pay and working conditions. There was severe hardship in the 1920s and 30s, when many people lost their jobs. By the 1980s many heavy industries, such as mining or steel manufacture, were closing down too. More workers were now women and many of them were employed in the service industries, such as banking or tourism, or in newer industries such as computer assembly.

HORSE POWER
Horses were used for deliveries of such things as coal and milk for much of the century.

AT THE PITHEAD
Until the 1980s, coal was the chief fuel of industry and power stations.

BOOM AND BUST

How should the world of work be organised? During the twentieth century there were two rival systems. Capitalist countries, such as the USA, supported private ownership of industry. This system survived major shocks in the 1920s and 30s. Communists, who first came to power in Russia in 1917, believed in public ownership and state control. However Russia returned to capitalism in 1991.

WAR WORK

During the First World War (1914-18) most young men were away in the army. Many factory jobs were taken for the first time by women workers.

MUNITIONS
A young woman assembles ammunition for use in World War I.

A HIGH OLD TIME
These New York construction workers had a head for heights!

TIMELINE

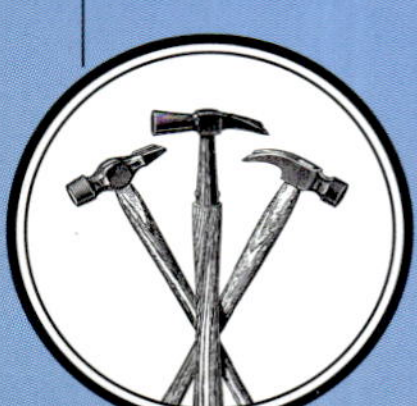

1900

1900 First offshore oilrig (USA)

1910

1913 Moving assembly line (USA)

1915 Women urged to work (UK)

1917 Communists seize power (Russia)

1920

1926 GeneraL Strike (UK)

1929 Wall Street Cash (USA)

1930

1930 2 million unemployed (UK)

1935 Dust storms destroy farms (USA)

1938 Motor combine harvesters (USA)

1940

1946 Hydraulic pit-props in mines (UK)

DOWN ON THE FARM
It was many years before tractors replaced horses.

NEW JOBS, NEW SKILLS
A telephone engineer fixes a line.

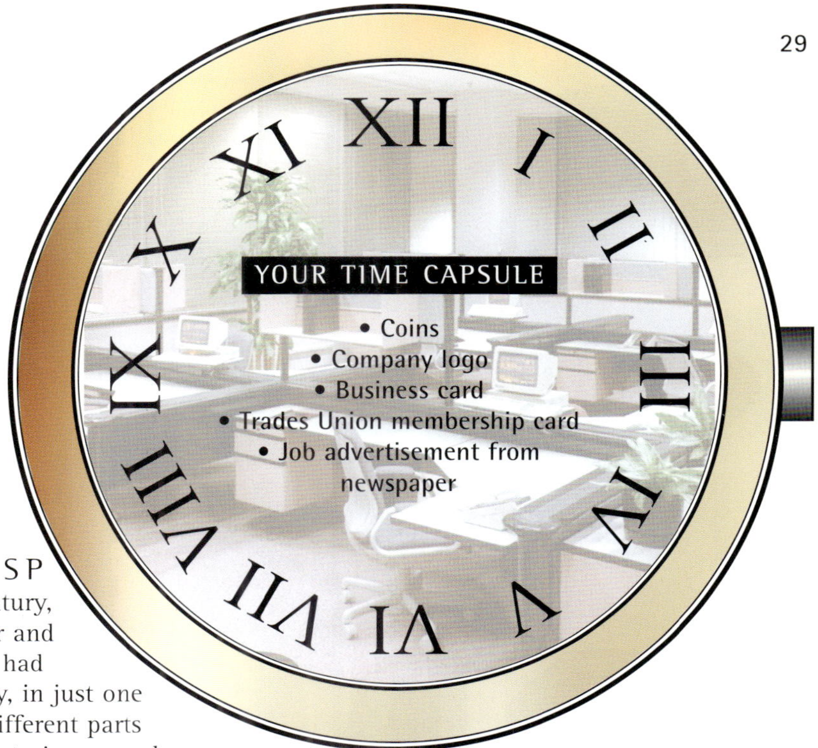

A CHANGING WORLD

Technology raced ahead in the twentieth century. Most of the working skills which were valuable at the start of the century were meaningless by the 1990s. Workers in almost all industries needed constant retraining. From the 1980s onwards personal computers made it possible for many more people to run businesses from their own homes. Factories were cleaner and less dangerous, but injuries at work were still all too common. Stress and strain increased in many jobs.

A GLOBAL GRASP

During the twentieth century, companies became larger and larger In the 1950s, cars had mostly been made locally, in just one country. By the 1990s, different parts might be supplied by factories around the world. Some transnational companies were now wealthier than individual countries.

LIFESAVER
A firefighter stands by, ready to attack a blaze. People still have to risk their lives for others.

PROTECT AND SURVIVE
Specialist clothing has been developed for new hazardous chemicals.

WHAT LIES AHEAD?
Will the next millennium bring harder working conditions or more leisure, as machines take over the jobs of humans?

950

53 Five-Year-Plan in ina to speed ustrialization

1960

1961 One millionth Morris Minor comes off production line (UK)

1970

1975 Yvonne Pope becomes first woman to captain a jet airline (UK)

1980

1983 Lech Walesa, Polish trade union leader, awarded Nobel Peace prize

1986 Nissan open a car assembly plant in northeast England (UK)

1990

1990s New regulations and working practices introduced by the EEC

2000

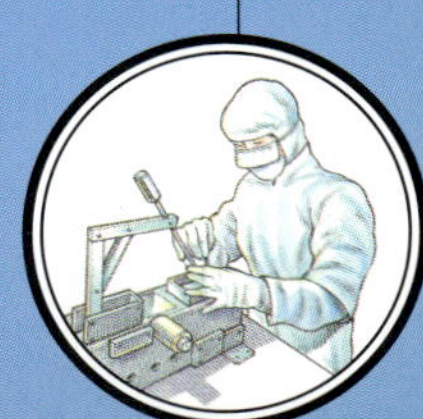

COMMUNICATION

MARCONI, RADIO PIONEER

On 11 December 1901 an Italian inventor, Guglielmo Marconi, sent a radio message across the Atlantic Ocean, from Cornwall, England, to Newfoundland.

At the end of the twentieth century, we take it all for granted... We watch news as it happens on the other side of the world. An Australian can telephone their friend in France as easily as the person next door. Faxes and e-mails send messages instantly. On television, we can see a humming-bird fly in slow motion, or watch a football goal being replayed from different angles. Back in 1900, these possibilities were undreamed of. News travelled slowly and glimpses of the outside world were provided by pictures in magazines. The communications revolution changed the way we live and the way we understand the world.

THE PRINTED PAGE

In the 1900s the chief form of communication was still the printed page. People relied on newspapers to find out what was going on. They wrote letters or postcards for most purposes. Typewriters were used mostly by businesses. Photocopiers were invented in 1938 and in the following year printers were setting type by a photographic process, rather than with metal. Computer-controlled laser printing was invented in Germany in 1965. Despite the popularity of radio and television, more and more books were published around the world.

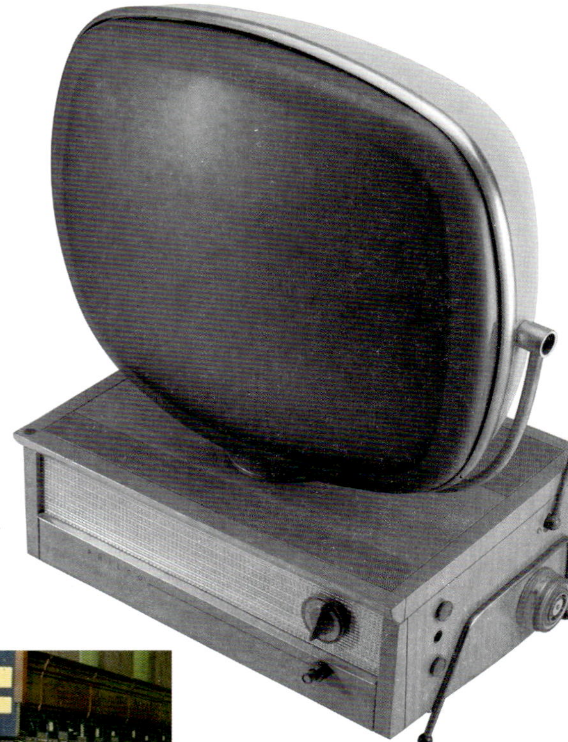

FUTURISTIC!

This television set from 1948 looked like no other. Its streamlined screen could be swivelled like a mirror.

THE HELLO GIRLS

Telephone exchanges became increasingly automated. By the late 1950s it was possible to dial long-distance direct.

TIMELINE

1900

1902 Electric typewriter (USA)

1904 Radio valve (UK)

1910

1916 Teleprinter (USA)

1917 AT&T introduces the world's first telex service for United Press (USA)

1920

1920 Regular radio broadcasts (USA)

1924 UK to Australia radio communication

1927 Trans-Atlantic telephone by radio (UK/USA)

1930

1935 Modern tape recorder (Germany)

1939 First television serial broadcast (USA)

1939 First televising of American football (USA)

1940

1940 Colour TV demonstrated (USA)

1947 Transistor (USA)

MEDIA POWER
Communications media such as newspapers, radio and television wielded great influence.

THE GLOBAL VILLAGE

In the 1960s, the world was already being described as a 'global village', meaning that rapid communications had put us all in touch with each other at the press of a button. Even then, most people failed to realise what would follow. The microprocessor chip, invented in the United States in 1969, led within six years to the first personal computer in the home. By the 1990s, the Internet – a worldwide information network in which telephone lines link up personal computers – really did make worldwide communication as easy as village gossip. That was the trouble, said some – too much gossip.

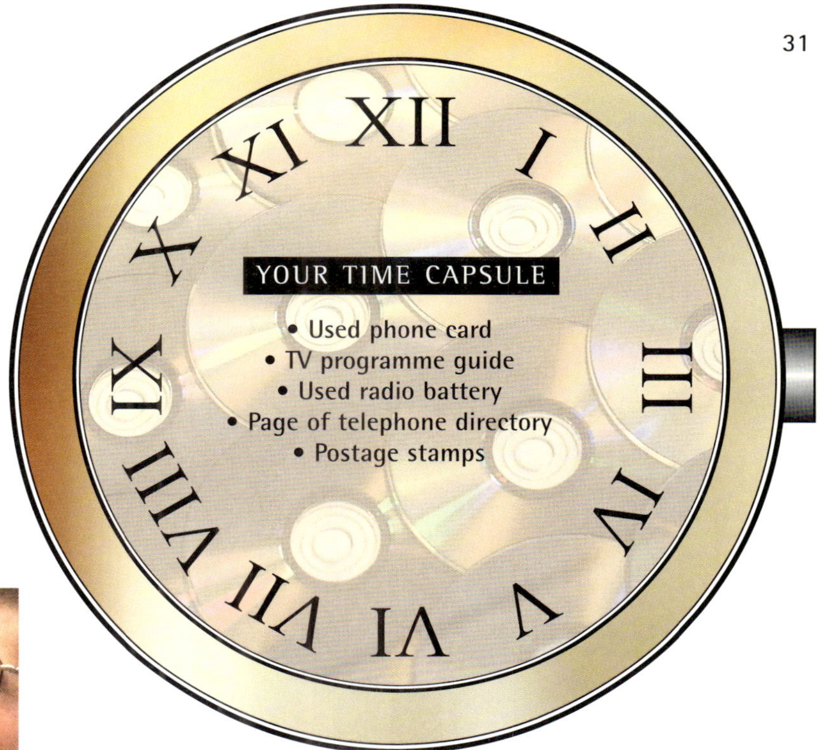

YOUR TIME CAPSULE

- Used phone card
- TV programme guide
- Used radio battery
- Page of telephone directory
- Postage stamps

MOBILE MANIA
By the 1990s mobile phones were all the rage.

TELSTAR AND AFTER

The first proper telecommunications satellite was Telstar, launched in 1962. It could broadcast telephone or television signals. Satellites now control many of Earth's communications systems. How long will it be before we can communicate with life forms on other planets?

GLOBAL TV
The World Cup in 1998 brought football matches to a world of armchair spectators.

BEAM ME UP!
Telephone, radio and television now send signals via space satellites.

COMPUTER CONTROL
From keyboard to voice commands to – chips implanted in the brain?

950

54 Transistor radio (USA)
56 Trans-Atlantic
ephone cable (UK/USA)

1960

1960 Satellite telephone
1963 Audio-cassette recorder (Netherlands)
1964 Word processor (USA)

1970

1971 Microprocessor
1973 Colour photocopier (Japan)

1980

1984 Mobile phone service (USA)
1985 CD-ROM
1987 Internet computer network

1990

1994 Annual phone calls pass 550 billion mark (USA)
1997 Fears voiced about millennium computer bug

2000

INVENTIONS

CLEVER BUT DEADLY
Tanks were first used in 1916 and were still delivering terror 80 years later.

A CENTURY OF TERROR

The twentieth century was an age of terrible warfare, mass murder, dictatorship and oppression. Inventors worked just as hard at producing weapons of destruction as they did at helping humanity. This was the century of the modern naval submarine (1900), the sub machine gun (1915), chemical warfare (1915), the tank (first used in 1916), the bomber plane (1916), the jet fighter (1941) and the ballistic missile (1942). The atomic bomb dropped on the Japanese city of Hiroshima in 1945 ended the Second World War, but killed 80,000 civilians and, injured 50,000.

Many inventions of our time have made our lives more convenient – the electric shaver (1928), say, or velcro fasteners (1948). Some have made our lives safer, such as 'cat's eye' reflectors on the roads (1934). Some inventions have been tasty, such as the choc ice or 'Eskimo pie' (1922) while others have been downright silly, such as the plastic 'hula hoop' of 1958. It did sell 20 million in the first six months, though! Some of the most fascinating inventions have helped us discover about the distant past, such as radio-carbon dating (1947) which can tell us just how old historical objects really are. The Hubble Space Telescope (1990) can look further into our Universe than ever before, recording visible light, ultra-violet and infra-red sources. Images from the edge of the known Universe take so long to reach us that the HST is recording events at the dawn of time.

START OF A NEW AGE
The first electronic computer (1946), was called ENIAC and weighed 30 tonnes.

TIMELINE

1900

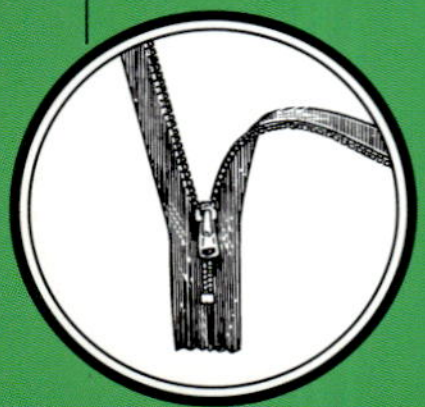

1906 Vacuum flask (UK)

1909 Bakelite (Belgium)

1910

1912 Cellophane (Switzerland)

1918 Sonar –Sound Navigation and Ranging (France)

1920

1925 First demonstration of television (UK)

1925 Adhesive tape (USA)

1926 Electron microscope (Germany)

1926 Aerosol (Norway)

1930

1930 Perspex – plastic glass (USA)

1936 Gas turbine (Switzerland)

1938 Ballpoint pen (Hungary)

1940

1940 Jeep (USA)

1942 Aqualung (France)

1946 Ballpoint pen goes on sale

HARNESSING THE ATOM
Nuclear reactors in USA. Nuclear power turned out to be more dangerous than was thought when the Chernobyl disaster happened.

YOUR TIME CAPSULE
- Your sketch of a future invention
- Felt-tip pen
- Disposable camera
- Audio/video cassette
- Compact disc
- Clippings from computers magazine

OUT OF THIS WORLD

In 1903 the Russian scientist Konstantin Tsiolkovsky published his theories of rocket propulsion and by 1926 an American, Robert Goddard, had launched a mini-rocket which used liquid fuels. In 1961 Russian cosmonaut Yuri Gagarin became the first human to be launched into Earth orbit. Science-fiction dreams came true as people landed on the Moon (1969) and space probes explored other planets. The Space Shuttle (1977) was launched into space by rockets, but could land like a plane, on a runway.

BLAST OFF
A Space Shuttle hitches a ride into space on the back of booster rockets.

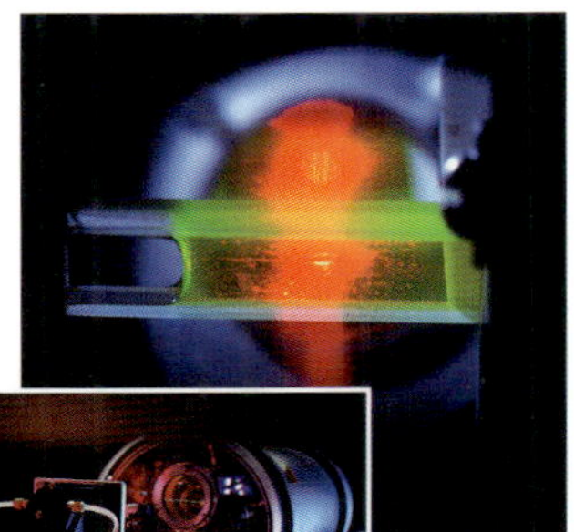

MAGIC BEAMS

Light Amplification by Stimulated Emission of Radiation – it was simpler to call it a 'laser'. The idea was proposed in the USA in 1958 and two years later the first machines had been made. Laser beams are light waves in which the wavelengths are made to be exactly the same, instead of being diffused. They can be used in surgery, in weapons, in printing, in making compact discs, in reading bar codes, in measuring instruments.

LASER POWER
The sheer power of a laser beam can cut rough steel.

DISPOSABLE
Throw-away was the motto of the century. We learned to use disposable cups, razors and nappies.

)50

52 Float glass process
K)

54 Non-stick pans
ance)

56 Battery powered
tch (USA)

1960

1963 Felt-tipped pen (Japan)

1970

1971 Pocket calculator (USA)

1975 Home computer (1975)

1980

1984 Hologram (USA)

1984 First domestic robot (USA)

1985 First mobile phones in UK introduced

1990

1990 Sony produce an electronic book called Data Discman

2000

ENTERTAINMENT

THE STAR
Italian-American Rudolph Valentino, heart-throb of the 1920s cinema.

Who was the most famous person in the world in the 1920s? A politician? A king, or a general? It was probably Charlie Chaplin, a British music hall comic who had gone to Hollywood, USA, to star in the silent movies. The cinema was the first great, exciting new entertainment of the century. The first talking film to be a smash hit was *The Jazz Singer* (1927), starring Al Jolson. Cartoon characters became as famous as film stars, with Felix the Cat (1917) followed by the great Mickey Mouse in the first cartoon talkie, *Steamboat Willie* (1928). The golden age of the cinema came in the 1940s and 50s, the age of Technicolor, cowboy films and musicals. Traditional art forms such as theatre and ballet survived the coming of cinema and took exciting new directions. In its turn, cinema survived the coming of its new rival, television.

POPCORN TIME
Saturday mornings in the 1950s, in the UK, was time for the 'pictures'.

ROLLERCOASTER!

Why do people like to make themselves sick and call it fun? It's hard to say. Yet from the very start of the century, everyone loved fairgrounds. Alongside traditional merry-go-rounds and swingboats were huge Ferris wheels and rollercoasters. By the 1990s these were hurling passengers around the track at speeds of up to 160 km per hour.

THE FUN OF THE FAIR
Permanent fairgrounds were set up at seaside resorts.

TIMELINE

1900

1902 Film special effects (France)

1910

1910 First Hollywood movie (USA)

1917 First jazz recording

1920

1925 Dodgem cars (UK)

1926 *d.* Harry Houdini, escapologist (USA

1926 First record by Bing Crosby (USA)

1930

1933 Stereo record (UK)

1933 Drive-in cinema (USA)

1936 Regular Black and white TV (USA)

1940

1942 Bing Crosby's White Christmas (USA)

1947 Long-playing record – LP (USA)

ANOTHER NICKEL
Electric jukeboxes were made from 1927, peaking in the rockin' 1950s.

SOUND SYSTEMS

The music lover of the early 1900s had a choice of the phonograph, which played wax cylinders, and the gramophone or record-player. LPs (long-playing records) appeared in 1947 and mini tape cassettes in 1963.By then, records were being made of vinyl. CDs(compact discs) went on the market in 1983, offering a clearer, more perfect sound.

YOUR TIME CAPSULE

- Pop music poster
- Theatre programme
- Old sheet music
- What's On page from a newspaper
- Audio cassette of music
- Brochure from museum, fun park, zoo etc.

ACROBATICS
The Chinese State Circus can still amaze us with traditional skills.

MUSIC FOR THE MASSES

The gramophone brought music to a far wider audience than ever before. Classical musicians now played for the recording studio as much as for the concert hall. Jazz and popular music both went through rapid variations which boosted record sales. The first US pop charts were published in 1936. The biggest stars? Elvis Presley in the 50s, the Beatles in the 60s.

ROCK AID
A rock concert raises money for strife-torn Bosnia in the 1990s.

REALITY (VIRTUALLY)
Virtual reality games, everyone thought, would take over. So far they have not.

950

951 Regular colour TV (USA)

952 CinemaScope wide-screen cinema (USA)

955 Disneyland theme park (USA)

1960

1961 Motown Records hits

1962 First Beatles hit (UK)

1970

1970 Bob Marley becomes international reggae star

1975 Home video system (Japan)

1979 'Walkman' personal stereo (Japan)

1980

1980 Pink Floyd's *The Wall* is worldwide hit

1984 First hit by Madonna

1990

1992 Digital TV (USA)

1995 Interactive cinema (USA)

2000

ENVIRONMENT

The chorus of a song which was popular in 1970 went: 'You don't know what you've got till it's gone'. Refrigerators, cars and power stations had all made our lives easier in the twentieth century. But people gradually began to realise that manufacture, mining and cutting down forests had severely damaged our planet. Roads had eaten up the countryside, more and more cars were belching out exhaust fumes. Foul smog hung over many cities. Even the rain was poisoned as it fell. Chemicals from factories and fertilisers from farms had poisoned rivers and killed fish. In the 1980s and 1990s the cleaning up process began. New laws were passed protecting wildlife and the countryside. But the planet as a whole was still suffering. Scientists now knew that the gases given out by industry and traffic were warming up the world's climate to dangerous levels.

A REAL PEA-SOUPER
Smog, a mixture of smoke and fog, was very common in London during the 1950s. It was said to be as thick as pea-soup. New laws cleaned up air in the English capital in the 1960s.

CLEAN AIR ACTS

The smoke from house fires, factory chimneys and exhaust fumes created London's worst ever smog in 1952. It choked the lungs and caused many accidents. A series of new laws were passed to clean up the environment and the city became a 'smokeless zone'. Today the city is a cleaner, healthier and sunnier place. Other cities around the world, from Athens to Mexico City to Los Angeles, still suffer from smog today.

TRAFFIC JAMS
One of the worst polluters was the lead in petrol. Lead-free petrol was sold from 1975.

ON SAFARI
European big-game hunters came to the African colonies to slaughter the wildlife there – for fun.

TIMELINE

1900

1902 American bison rescued from extinction (USA)

1910

1911 Newfoundland white wolf extinct

1914 Passenger pigeon extinct (USA)

1920

1921 Aerial pesticides (USA)

1930

1933 Tasmanian wolf extinct (Australia)

1934 Dustbowl soil erosion (USA)

1939 DDT, a dangerous pesticide (Switzerland)

1940

1948 Founding of International Union for Conservation of Nature (UN)

ENERGY PROBLEMS
A flare burns off oil surplus. Oil and coal are fossil fuels. As sources of energy, they cannot be renewed and are heavy polluters. Nuclear fuel is clean, but expensive and extremely dangerous in the event of an accident. Since the 1980s renewable energy has been tried out – from the sun, wind and tides.

VANISHING HERDS
The African elephant found its habitat taken for farms and its routes blocked by roads.

YOUR TIME CAPSULE

- Weather forecast from newspaper
- Leaf or bark rubbings
- Birds' feathers
- Postcards of wild animals
- Dustbin liner/list of rubbish
- Bottle for recycling

CROP CONTROL
Pesticides help the farmer but they may poison rivers and kill wildlife

WILDLIFE HAVENS

The idea of setting aside land to preserve wildlife and the environment, began in the United States in the 1870s. Today, most countries have national parks where endangered animals can live freely, protected by game wardens. The tourists attracted to these parks can help to pay for their upkeep. Tigers and Asiatic lions are preserved in India, Nepal and Bangladesh, rhinoceroses and elephants in Africa and orang-utans in Southeast Asia. Many reserves are still threatened by poachers and hunters, profiting from the illegal trade in ivory, furs, hides and captive birds and animals.

RECYCLE YOUR WASTE

From the 1970s, many people became more conscious of environmental, or 'green' issues. They wanted to save increasingly precious resources. In the home, families saved paper, glass, cans and old clothes. These were left at collecting points in many towns, and taken away for recycling.

USE IT AGAIN!
Newspapers and bottles are crated up for recycling.

FASHION STATEMENT
In the 1970s animal furs were out – and fake fur was in.

950

952 Clean Air Act (UK)

954 First nuclear power ation (Russia)

954 Solar cells (USA)

1960

1964 Bio-degradable washing powder (Germany)

1968 First 'green' movement (USA)

1968 Tidal power station (France)

1970

1974 Ozone depletion in Earth's atmosphere

1975 Lead-free petrol on sale (USA)

1980

1983 Green party political success (Germany)

1988 Global warming confirmed

1989 Bio-degradable plastic (Italy)

1990

1992 Earth summit, Rio de Janeiro

1997 Forest fires across SE Asia

2000

ACHIEVEMENTS

VOTES FOR WOMEN
After long years of campaigning, American women gained the federal vote in 1920.

POLAR CHALLENGE
In the 1900s, explorers pushed to the last uncharted parts of Earth. The Norwegian Roald Amundsen was the first person to reach the South Pole, in 1911. He just beat the British explorer Robert F. Scott, who died on the return journey

How should the twentieth century be remembered? For its terrible wars, or for its attempts to bring peace to a troubled world? For its destructiveness or for its creativity? For its many tragedies or for its sense of fun? Every age has its evil aspects and its good aspects. What we often remember best from previous ages are individual acts of heroism or endurance. We remember people who succeeded in doing something that nobody had done before. We remember people who have struggled against injustice. Many such people lived in the last 100 years and many of them are already famous names. However, many of them are less well known. They are the millions of ordinary people who survived war and hard times and managed as best as they could. They might well include your own ancestors, who created the world you live in today.

THE WOMEN'S STRUGGLE

In the late 1800s, women in many western countries had struggled for the right to vote in national elections. Women voted for the first time in New Zealand in 1893, in Britain in 1918. The first woman prime minister was Sri Lankan Sirimavo Bandaranaike in 1960. From the 1960s and 70s women campaigned for equality in the home and at work.

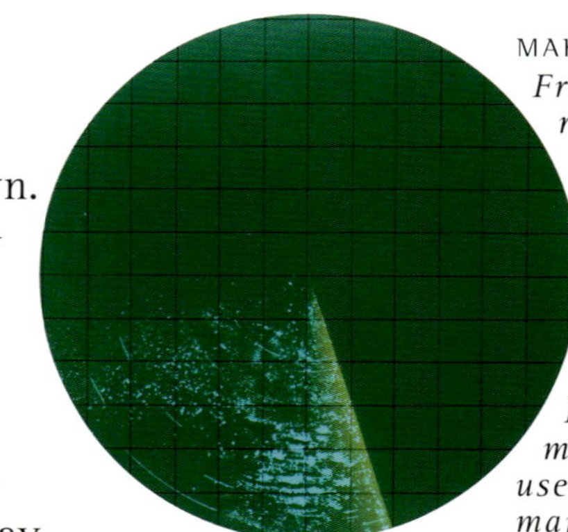

MAKING WAVES
From 1940, radar (Radio Detection and Ranging) used radio waves to detect objects such as planes. Radar had many other uses, such as mapping.

TIMELINE

1900

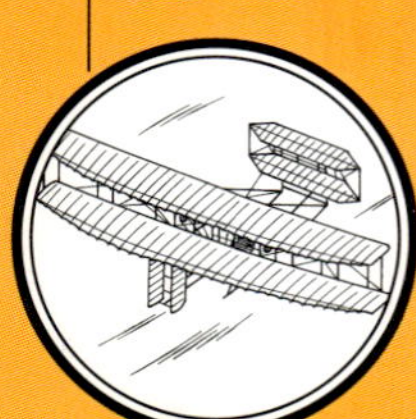

1900 Sigmund Freud's theory of dreams

1910

1913 Structure of the atom discovered (Denmark)

1915 Einstein's General Theory of Relativity (Germany)

1920

1922 First diabetic to be treated with insulin (Canada).

1930

1930 Amy Johnson (UK) flies Britain to Australia solo

1932 Amelia Earhart (US) first woman to fly Atlantic solo

1940

1943 First electronic computer (UK).

1947 Kon Tiki raft voyage (Pacific)

LET IT RIP!
Richard Noble's Thrust 2 speeds over Black Rock Desert, Nevada, USA, at a speed of 1,019.467 km per hour, in 1983. Back in 1903, the land speed record had stood at just 210.2 km per hour.

YOUR TIME CAPSULE

- Headlines from newspapers
- Famous autographs you have collected
- Badges
- Certificates for swimming, sports etc.

SERVING HUMANITY

The century may have been restless and destructive, but it was also a time of international cooperation, with the founding of the League of Nations (1919) and the United Nations (1945). Many individuals struggled for justice and fought racism and inequality. This was an age of education and artistic creativity. It was an age of scientific discovery and lifesaving medical advances.

RECORD BREAKERS

On 6 May 1954 an English athlete called Roger Bannister became the first person to run a mile (1.6 kilometres) in under 4 minutes – 3 minutes 59.4 seconds to be precise. Throughout the century, the records kept falling. There were many reasons – professional training, improved equipment and a scientific approach all played their part. But the most important factor was the human spirit, the desire to push oneself to the limits.

KEYHOLE SURGERY
As we looked out into space, we also looked inwards, exploring our own bodies.

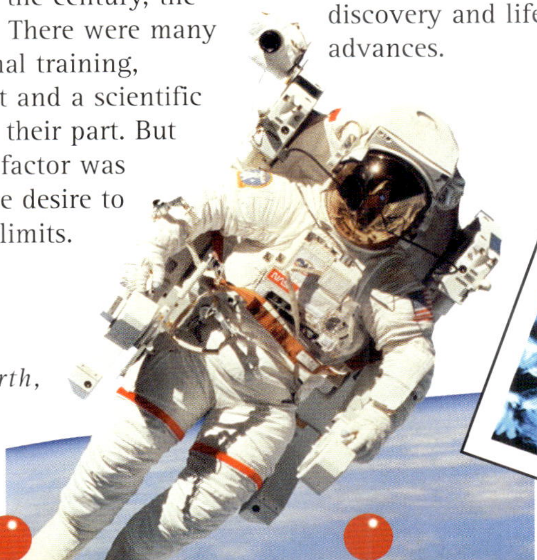

SPACE FEATS
High above the Earth, astronaut Bruce McCandless manoeuvres his support unit.

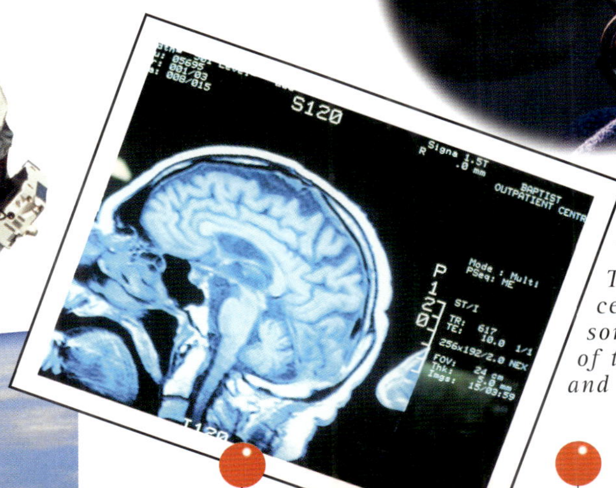

BRAINWAVES
The twentieth century brought us some understanding of the human brain and how it functions.

950

953 Mt Everest climbed Jepal/NZ)

957 First undersea voyage eneath North Pole by US ıbmarine.

1960

1961 Yuri Gagarin (USSR) first man in space

1963 Valentina Tereshkova first woman in space

1965 Space walk (USSR)

1970

1972 Pioneer 10 spacecraft blasts off for Jupiter.

1977 Soviet ship Arkitka is first surface vessel to reach the North Pole

1980

1988 Kay Cottee (Australia) first woman to sail around the world solo

1990

1992 Solo Antarctic crossing Boerge Ousland (Norway)

2000

CHRONOLOGY

1900 Victor Emmanuel III King of Italy. Founding of Labour Party, UK. War in South Africa. Famine in India. Rebellion in China.

1901 Commonwealth of Australia founded. Queen Victoria dies, Edward VII King (UK). US President McKinley shot, Theodore Roosevelt takes over.

Queen Victoria. With her death an era ended and a century began.

1902 Cuban independence. End to war in South Africa. Mt Pelée erupts, Martinique, 30,000 killed.

1903 Typhoid, New York. Turks massacre Bulgarians.

1904 Japan defeats Russia. Herero people rise against Germans in Southwest Africa (Namibia).

1905 Revolution in Russia forces reform. Albert Einstein publishes theories about the Universe.

1906 San Francisco earthquake. Typhoon kills 10,000 in Tahiti. Volcanic eruption of Mt Vesuvius, Italy.

1907 Votes for women, Norway. Finns elect women MPs.

1908 King Carlos I of Portugal assassinated. Sicilian earthquake. Franco-British Exhibition at White City, London.

1909 Revolt in Turkey. William Howard Taft becomes US President.

1910 Republic of South Africa founded. Revolution in Portugal. Death of King Edward VII, UK.

1911 China overthrows last emperor. Revolution in Mexico. George V crowned, UK.

Titanic sinks!

1912

1912 China becomes a republic. Christian X becomes King of Denmark. The new liner *Titanic* sinks in North Atlantic. Woodrow Wilson becomes US President.

1913 War in the Balkans. King George I of Greece assassinated.

1914 Austrian Archduke assassinated in Balkans. Start of the First World War, with British Empire, France and Russia fighting Germany and Austria.

1915 Massive casualties in War. Italy

FIRST ZEPPELIN SHOT DOWN

1915

declares war on Austria. Submarine warfare, passenger liner *Lusitania* sunk by German torpedoes.

1916 Easter Rising suppressed by British troops in Ireland. Arab revolt against Turkish rule.

1917 USA enters War. Tsar overthrown in Russia, Kerensky head of state. October Revolution in Russia, Lenin's Bolsheviks seize power.

1918 Over 21 million killed by influenza worldwide. First World War ends.

1919 Treaty of Versailles settles terms of peace. Communist insurrections in Germany. German Nazi party founded.

The invention of the tank dramatically changed tactics in the First World War.

00 1910 1920 1930 1940 1950 1960 1970 1980 1990

1920 Baltic States independent. Civil war in Russia. Irish Republican Army battles with British troops.

1921 Rif War in Morocco. Famine in Russia.

1922 Benito Mussolini becomes Fascist dictator in Italy. Calvin Coolidge becomes US President. Russia renamed USSR (Union of Soviet Socialist Republics, or Soviet Union).

1923 Mustapha Kemal 'Atatürk' President of Turkey.

Tomb of Tutankhamun FOUND

1922

1924 Death of Russian leader Lenin, Joseph Stalin takes his place.

1925 Death of Chinese leader Sun Yat-sen, replaced by General Chiang Kai-shek.

1926 Hirohito becomes Emperor of Japan.

1927 Saudi Arabia independent. In USSR, Stalin expels opponents, including Leon Trostsky, from the Communist Party.

1928 Herbert Hoover becomes US President.

1929 Economic crisis in USA.

John Logie Baird began his pioneering work on television in the 1920s.

1930 World financial crisis. Military coup in Argentina. Revolution in Brazil. Haile Selassie Emperor of Ethiopia. Ghandi's Salt March (India)

1931 Japan invades eastern China. Gangster Al Capone imprisoned (USA).

1932 FD Roosevelt becomes US President. Antonio Salazar becomes dictator in Portugal. Democratic reform in Siam (Thailand).

1933 Nazi leader Adolf Hitler becomes German Chancellor.

1934 'Long March' of Chinese communists under Mao Zedong in fight against nationalists.

1935 Italy invades Ethiopia. Dust storms destroy farmland in USA, great hardship.

BLUEBIRD sets new landspeed record

1935

1936 Stalin purges opponents in USSR, 10 million die. Spanish Civil War begins. In UK, George V dies, King Edward VIII abdicates.

1937 Guernica bombed in Spanish Civil War. Europe prepares for wider conflict.

1938 Germany annexes Austria. Britain and France give in to Hitler's demand for the Sudetenland, in Czechoslovakia. Terrible persecution of Jews in Germany.

1939 General Francisco Franco wins Spanish Civil War and becomes dictator. Germany invades Poland. Start of Second World War, as Britain and France declare war on Germany.

American Amelia Earhart flew solo across the Atlantic in 1932.

1940 Germany invades Norway and Denmark. Winston Churchill becomes British Prime Minister. Germany invades Belgium, France. General Charles de Gaulle forms Free French government in exile. Air warfare in Battle of Britain. Italy, Germany and Japan form alliance.

Japan **BOMBS** *Pearl Harbour*

1941

1941 Germany invades Greece, Yugoslavia, USSR. Ethiopia regains independence. Japan bombs Pearl Harbour. USA joins War.

1942 Japan invades Southeast Asia. Tank warfare in North Africa. Battle for Stalingrad, in USSR – over 1.5 million casualties.

1943 Naval warfare in Pacific. Mass murder of Jews in Nazi occupied Europe – the Holocaust. Allies invade Italy.

1944 D-Day landings, Allies invade occupied France, Belgium.

1945 USSR takes Central Europe, meet Allied troops in Germany. Germany surrenders. USA drops atomic bombs on Japan. Japan surrenders, end of Second World War.

1946 United Nations Organisation founded. Italy becomes republic. War criminals tried at Nuremberg, Germany.

1947 India becomes independent under Jawaharlal Nehru. Strife over partition with Pakistan. 'Cold War' starts between Soviet Union and West.

1948 Burma becomes independent. Gandhi is assassinated in India. Soviet forces in Germany try to blockade traffic to Berlin. The Berlin Airlift – west flies in supplies.

1949 Communist defeat Nationalists in China, declare a People's Republic. Ireland becomes a full republic.

1950 Riots against racist laws passed in South Africa. USSR has atomic weapons. Communist troops from North Korea invade South Korea, start of Korean War. United Nations force captures south. Chinese troops invade Tibet.

1951 Spy scandals in USA and UK.

Gas guzzlers of the 1950s. Cars became more affordable after the war.

1952 Dwight Eisenhower becomes US President. British King George VI dies. Kenyan 'Maumau' terror campaign against British colonials.

1953 Major uranium discovery, Canada. Joseph Stalin dies in USSR. Coronation of Elizabeth II (UK).

Everest conquered

1953

1954 Gamal Abdel Nasser comes to power in Egypt. Anti-communist witch hunt in USA. French battle with Vietnamese at Dien Bien Phu. Geneva Conference agrees borders in Vietnam.

1955 Anthony Eden becomes British Prime Minister. Military coup in Argentina.

1956 Independence for Sudan, Morocco, Tunisia. Nasser nationalises Suez Canal, France and Britain send in troops. Rebellion against Soviet power in Hungary. Crisis in Cyprus as rebels demand union with Greece,

1957 China's 'Great Leap Forward', country organised into communes. Harold Macmillan becomes British Prime Minister. European Economic Community founded.

Buddy Holly DIES in Air Crash

1959

1958 US submarine sails underneath North Pole. General Charles de Gaulle becomes French president as French colony of Algeria revolts.

1959 Cuban dictator Fulgencio Batista flees as Fidel Castro gains power. Castro visits Washington. Singapore gains independence.

1960 17 African countries gain independence. South African police massacre protestors, Sharpeville. Civil war in Congo. John Kennedy becomes US President.

GAGARIN first man in SPACE

1961

1961 Soviet Union launches man into space. Invasion of exiles with US backing defeated at Bay of Pigs, Cuba. Berlin, Germany, divided by wall. Campaign for Nuclear Disarmament, UK.

1962 World on brink of nuclear war as USA and USSR stand off over Soviet missile sites in Cuba. Fighting on India-China border.

Jackie Kennedy was an icon in her time. She influenced fashion in the 1960s.

1963 Political scandal in UK. Pop music culture. Struggle for Black civil rights in southern United States, led by Martin Luther King. Assassination of US President John Kennedy. Lyndon B Johnson becomes President.

1964 Freedom fighter Nelson Mandela jailed for life, South Africa. USA commits itself to Vietnam conflict. Harold Wilson British Prime Minister.

1965 US planes bomb North Vietnam. US troops join ground war amidst growing protests. India fights Pakistan in Kashmir. Crisis in Rhodesia (modern Zimbabwe).

1966 Indira Gandhi Indian Prime Minister. Cultural Revolution in China.

1967 Israel wins Six Day War against Arabs. War in Biafra, West Africa. Anti-Vietnam war protests.

NIXON elected US president

1968

1968 Martin Luther King assassinated, USA. Student and worker uprising in France. Soviet tanks crush reforms in Czechoslovakia. Richard Nixon becomes US President.

1969 Northern Ireland's Catholics demand civil rights. US astronauts land on Moon.

1970 US troops invade Cambodia. Anti-war protestors shot in Ohio, USA. Edward Heath becomes UK Prime Minister. Palestinian terrorists hijack jets and blow them up. Anwar Sadat becomes Egyptian President.

First JUMBO JET arrives at Heathrow

1970

1971 Women's liberation campaigns. Internment without trial in Northern Ireland. Attica prison revolt, New York. India defeats Pakistan in war over East Pakistan (Bangladesh).

1972 Bangladesh becomes independent. Provisional IRA bombs England. Massive US bombing of North Vietnam. Palestinian terrorists attack Israel Olympic team at Munich.

1973 UK and Ireland join European Economic Community. USA pulls troops out of Vietnam. Democratically elected President Salvador Allende murdered in Chilean coup. General Pinochet siezes power. Yom Kippur War in Israel. Spanish Prime Minister killed by Basque bomb.

Towards the end of the century the Panda joined the endangered species list.

Elvis dies

1977

1974 Military rule ends in Greece. US President Nixon resigns over Watergate scandal.

1975 Khmer Rouge forces under Pol Pot conquer Cambodia. North Vietnam conquers South Vietnam, panic at US Embassy. Portugal holds democratic elections. Civil wars in Lebanon and Angola. Spain becomes monarchy.

1976 Uprising in Soweto, South Africa. Mao Zedong dies in China. Jimmy Carter becomes US President. Punk rock fashion.

1977 Spain holds democratic elections. Death of Elvis Presley, rock n' roll icon.

1978 Italian statesman Aldo Moro kidnapped and murdered by Red Brigade terrorists. Egyptian-Israeli peace treaty. John Paul 11 becomes Pope.

1979 Shah of Iran overthrown. Vietnam invades Cambodia, discover mass graves. Margaret Thatcher becomes Prime Minister in UK. Sandanista rebels overthrow Nicaraguan dictator. USSR invades Afghanistan. Peace in Zimbabwe.

1980 Mt St Helens volcanic eruption, Washington State, USA. Hostage taking at London's Iranian embassy. Polish workers found Solidarity opposition. Ronald Reagan becomes US President. Rock star John Lennon assassinated in New York.

1981 Attempted coup in Spain. Riots in Brixton district of London and other cities. François Mitterand becomes French President. President Sadat of Egypt is assassinated, Hosni Mubarak takes his place. Church of England admits women priests.

Prince Charles and Lady Di MARRY

1981

1982 3 million unemployed in UK. Argentina invades British colony of the Falkland Islands. Britain recaptures islands. Bitter fighting in Beirut, Lebanon. Greenham Common peace camp, UK.

Iran-Iraq war

1983

00 1910 1920 1930 1940 1950 1960 1970 1980 1990

Lady Di, the People's Princess, is taken to the hearts of admirers worldwide.

1983 Iran-Iraq War. US invades Grenada.

1984 AIDS virus discovered. Miners' strike, UK. Indian troops battle with Sikh separatists. Indira Gandhi assassinated, India. Famine in Ethiopia.

1985 Mikhail Gorbachev becomes leader in USSR. 'Live Aid' rock concerts raise funds for Ethiopian famine victims. French agents blow up vessel of Greenpeace, an ecological organisation, in New Zealand.

1986 US Space Shuttle explodes. Swedish Prime Minister Olof Palme is assassinated. USA bombs Libya. Chernobyl nuclear disaster in USSR.

1987 Ferry *Herald of Free Enterprise* sinks in North Sea. Cold War ends as West's relations with the USSR improve. Iranian Moslems riot at Mecca during annual pilgrimage. Black Monday – London Stock Market crash.

1988 Oil rig fire in North Sea. Floods in Bangladesh. George Bush becomes US President. Jumbo jet is blown up over Scottish town of Lockerbie.

1989 Soviet Union begins to break up. Berlin Wall knocked down in Germany.

1990 Saddam Hussein, leader of Iraq, invades Kuwait.

1991 Gulf War forces Iraq out of Kuwait. Germany reunified under Chancellor Helmut Kohl. Free elections in former communist countries of Central Europe and Balkans. USSR dissolved, becomes the Russian federation, with Boris Yeltsin as President.

Oil was the main issue that inflamed the Gulf War in 1991.

1992 John Major becomes British Prime Minister. Bill Clinton becomes US President. Civil war in Somalia, US troops intervene. Break up of Yugoslavia. Start of widespread conflict in the Balkans.

1993 Israel agrees to peace process with Palestinians.

1994 North American Free Trade Agreement (USA, Mexico and Canada). End of racist government system in South Africa. US troops invade Haiti.

After long imprisonment, South Africa's Nelson Mandela was released in 1990.

1995 Jacques Chirac becomes French President.

1996 Continuing conflict in Balkans.

1997 Tony Blair becomes British Prime Minister. Peace agreement in Northern Ireland. Scotland and Wales vote for devolution of power within UK. Forest fires across Southeast Asia.

1998 Gerhard Schröder becomes German Chancellor. Instabilty of world stock markets. Major hurricane devastates Honduras and Nicaragua.

2000
HUGE MILLENNIUM PARTY

INDEX

ACKNOWLEDGEMENTS

Page 6 NASA; Page 8 (B/L) Hulton Deutsch/Corbis; (T/R) Dover Publications; Page 9 (B/L) Rex Features; (B/R) Laura Dwight/Corbis; Page 10 (T/R) Corbis-Bettmann; (B) Dover Publications: (T/C) courtesy Virgin Management Ltd.; (B/C) UPI/Bettmann/Corbis; Page 12 (T/R) Hulton Deutsch/Corbis; (B/R) Oscar White/Corbis; (C) UPI/Corbis-Bettmann; (B/R) courtesy Nike; Page 14 (T/L) Dover Publications; (B/R) courtesy Hasbro; Page 15 (C) courtesy Robert Bosch Ltd.; (B/R) Corbis; Page 18 (T/L) Hulton Deutsch/Corbis; Page 20 (T/L) Dover Publications; Page 21 (B) Elizabeth Whiting Agency; (B/R) R.Hyett/EWA/Corbis; Page 22 (T/L) Hulton Deutsch/Corbis; (B/R) courtesy Ford Motor Co.; Page 23 (B/L) Dean Conger/Corbis; (B/R) courtesy Honda; Page 24 (T/L) Dover Publications; (B/R) Corbis-Bettmann; Page 25 (B/L) Hulton Deutsch/Corbis; (B/C & B/R) The Stock Market; Page 26 (T/L) & (B/L) courtesy J. Sainsbury plc; (T/R) courtesy Cadbury Ltd.; (B/C) Hulton Deutsch/Corbis; Page 27 (R) courtesy Marks & Spencer; Page 28 (T/R) Hulton Deutsch/Corbis; (B/L) Hulton Deutsch/Corbis; Page 31 (B/L) Rex Features; Page 32 (T/L) Peter Sarson; (B/R) UPI/Corbis-Bettmann; Page 34 (T/R) Hulton Deutsch/Corbis; Page 35 (B/C) Rex Features; (B/R) Richard T. Nowitz/Corbis; Page 36 (T/C) Hulton Deutsch/Corbis; (B/R) Hulton Deutsch/Corbis; Page 38 (T/L) Corbis-Bettmann; Page 39 (T/L) UPI/Corbis-Bettmann; (T/C) courtesy Castrol International

All other photographs come from the MKP Archives

The publishers would like to thank John Woodcock and Aziz Khan for the artwork in this book.